Allez les Verts

# FC FOOTBALL GRAPHICS

# FC FOOTBALL GRAPHICS

JEREMY LESLIE AND PATRICK BURGOYNE

WITH 380 COLOUR ILLUSTRATIONS

THAMES AND HUDSON

# CONTENTS

# INTRODUCTION

**FOOTBALL IS THE WORLD'S GAME.** 170 countries entered the competition to qualify for the 1998 World Cup finals in France. What was once the simple pastime of the urban working classes has become a multi-billion pound, global leisure industry.

No other sport comes close to matching football's popularity and no other sport has such a vibrant, diverse culture attached to it. To those that follow it, football is far more than just a game: it is a way of life with its own iconography, its own symbolism.

From pitch markings to team strips and from match programmes to club badges, football has created its own coherent graphic language over the last century that transcends national and cultural boundaries. There are certain colours – royal blue, scarlet, white – which are football colours, others – pink, brown, grey – are not. Certain graphic styles – stripes, hoops, quarters – are football styles, others – chevrons, triangles, zig-zags – are not. Part heraldic, part tribal, these stylings have emerged, for the most part, independently of the design industry.

Nonetheless, what has come from the grass roots is graphically very exciting, sparking the interest of the creative community worldwide.

Football has also influenced fashion, music, advertising, art... even literature. Its sense of a coherent visual language rooted in popular culture has proved a fertile source of inspiration for creative people the world over. British fashion designers Paul Smith and Vivienne Westwood have used footballing references in their clothes. For the summer of 1997, Smith created a range of t-shirts featuring stills from football matches, as well as a range of leisure shirts whose striped fabric and styling mimicked that of football shirts – they even had the word "Swoosh" emblazoned across the chest in the manner of a sponsor's logo. In turn, Giorgio Armani designed the Italian team's off-field wear for the 1994 World Cup, Bruce Oldfield was commissioned to design the 1997/98 strip for Norwich City and footballers such as Liverpool's David James, Spurs' David Ginola and ex-Manchester United star Eric Cantona have made regular appearances as fashion models.

Graphic designers and advertising creatives have explored footballing imagery extensively in their work, using the game's hold on the public in the service of all manner of products. In one notable example, Me Company intimated the super-heroic status of players in fans' eyes by turning several Dutch stars into computer games characters in an ad campaign for Nike. Photographers, too, have been drawn to the game. Nadav Kander has taken a series of studies of the township game in South Africa, Julian Germain is involved in an ongoing project in the *favelas* of Brazil and Robert Wilson (son of former Arsenal keeper Bob) has produced a book of portraits of goalkeepers.

Director Gregory Rood, while at Tomato, made a 50-minute documentary about Brazilian star Romario in 1995. Rood titled the film *Campo Dourado*. Far from being a straight fly-on-the-wall treatment, it explored the status that Romario enjoyed among his countrymen after helping the national team win the World Cup in 1994. Romario was pictured being borne aloft by adoring fans carrying candles in a deliberately religious reference. Explaining why he was drawn to making a film on a footballer, Rood said that "it gave me a unique opportunity to look at the function of a demi-god in a society".

This interest in the role of football has also been heavily explored in literature: French existentialist Albert Camus attributed his knowledge of morality to the game, while more recently there has been a spate of new British writings, such as the *Book of Two Halves* and *Albion Rovers* collections and Nick Hornby's *Fever Pitch*. In the art world, too, "football is a source of ideas and imagery for contemporary artists", according to John Gill, curator of the *Offside* exhibition. *Offside* is a British touring exhibition around the theme of football and featuring the work of 13 artists from Argentina, Britain, Colombia and Mexico, including Simon Patterson, Mark Wallinger and Nick Waplington. Gill says: "Artists are using football to articulate ideas about life and the world we live in. They are using their passion for the game to open up other ideas like nationalism, commercialisation, fanaticism. As soon as you set two teams against each other, it becomes a metaphor for so much else. You have two warring factions. The teams wear colours. The opposing groups of supporters also wear those colours. These fans come together under their colours just as they did in wars in previous centuries. Football has a huge breadth of interest for the artist."

On a more commercial level, football has become big business as clubs have woken up to the vast incomes that can be generated from preying on fans' loyalties via marketing and merchandising. To maximise revenues, clubs have begun to turn away from their traditional customers in a bid to attract the affluent middle classes. In order to do

this they have had to spend millions overhauling dilapidated stadia, creating an environment suitable for a family audience. More architects, designers and marketing specialists are being brought in every day to update football's image. Drawing on the game's roots, they are reinterpreting footballing imagery for the modern consumer.

Following football now is a journey through a highly targeted marketing experience. Before a game, fans can keep up with their heroes through one of the thousands of football sites which have recently sprung up on the internet. Television is full of football-related commercials. Everything at the stadium itself is now branded by the club. From the pre-match burger to the match programme and from the half-time cuppa to the video information screens which are now a feature at many grounds, everything is tied in to the visual language of football. After the game a huge amount of media coverage via television, radio, newspapers and magazines is available, as well as celebrations of the game in books, films and music.

The football merchandising business is estimated to be worth £3 billion a year and shows no signs of slowing down. For the 1997/98 season Chelsea invested £2.5 million in building a three-storey, 10,500 square feet megastore – the biggest in Britain. Chelsea branded goods on offer include a watch at £29.99, a mountain bike at £249.99 and a scooter at £2,500. Italian giant Inter Milan has a fan magazine which offers supporters the opportunity to buy an Inter TV remote control, Inter car seat covers or, for the other love of your life, lacey Inter garters. Barcelona fans can drink from a mug which plays the club song or relax in Barça bubble bath.

Writing about replica kits in Britain's *Observer* newspaper, Andrew Anthony said: "the English psyche is no longer clothed in a Morris dancer's outfit but in what Freud might have called polyester perversity". He might just as easily have been talking about the Dutch or the Germans or any other soccer-mad country. A survey of Europe's popular holiday resorts will find hordes of men (and women) showing off their national and local allegiances via their preferred replica shirt.

In order to satisfy demand – or milk consumers for all their worth depending on how you look at it – clubs change their strip every two years. As they have up to four strips on the go at any one time, this usually results in at least one new design per season. To keep this up, the manufacturers' designers have had to tweak and twist a team's original stripes or colours out of all recognition in order to come up with something new each time. The original shirt designs have become so abstracted and been stripped of so much meaning that often the most distinguishing characteristic of a team's on-field identity is its sponsor's name. If it's Sharp

From top: shrine to AC Bilbao in Bullas, Spain; teaser poster for the film of Nick Hornby's *Fever Pitch*; private view invitation for the Offside exhibition, designed to look like a match ticket; t-shirt by Paul Smith; a souvenir match book from Italia 90 showing the strip of winners West Germany; The Chelsea Megastore.

it must be Man Utd, if it's JVC it must be Arsenal. The rest of the shirt could belong to anyone.

Somehow, in the days when shirts sported a standardised, limited set of traditional non-branded designs – stripes, hoops, halves – it didn't matter if a Southampton shirt looked the same as a Sheffield United shirt or that Bayern Munich looked the same as Liverpool. But now shirt design has left that rigid, codified world behind. In order to ensure that only the official, licensed kit is bought by fans, alien, individualistic visual devices have been introduced that do not belong to the world of hoops and halves. There are chevrons on shoulders, distorted stripes, shadings and zig-zags, pinstripes and diamonds. Now it *does* matter when Olympiques Lyons look like Anderlecht or when, except for a different neck, Sweden's shirt is the same as Romania's or when Karlsruhe's home shirt is the same as Burnley's away kit. Whereas the old kits seemed as if they had simply evolved from some kind of 100 per cent cotton primordial swamp, these new shirts are all-too-obviously the product of human hand. It is painful for fans to find out that their team is not important enough to warrant an exclusive design.

A few clubs have remained above this multicolour scramble for quick profit. The Milanese giants AC and Internazionale have stuck rigidly to their traditional red and black and blue and black stripes for their home shirts, despite the fact that they still alter the design every other season or so and are just as commercially aware as British clubs. Changes are minimal, being left to collar and cuff stylings or material. The true fan, it seems, will still need to buy the latest shirt even if it is only very slightly different from the old one. These giants of Serie A believe that their colours are sacrosanct as powerful symbols of tradition.

Perhaps learning from their Italian counterparts, British clubs, arguably bearers of the most outlandish stylings, appear to have realised that traditional designs have more resonance. Shirts have begun to return to more traditional graphic devices, meeting a demand that became obvious with the large sales of reissued "classic" kits from the sixties and seventies.

The visual language of football has won through because of all its associated meanings and memories. That is what makes it so powerful. That is why a real football stadium like the Luigi Ferraris in Genoa or the Bernabeu in Madrid will always have so much more atmosphere than a multi-purpose arena shared by other sports.

As John Gill says: "Football is not just about the game but about so much else. The passion for football is informed by life itself."

This book is an exploration of what it means to be a football fan in the approach to the millennium. Football is everywhere. It is part of life.

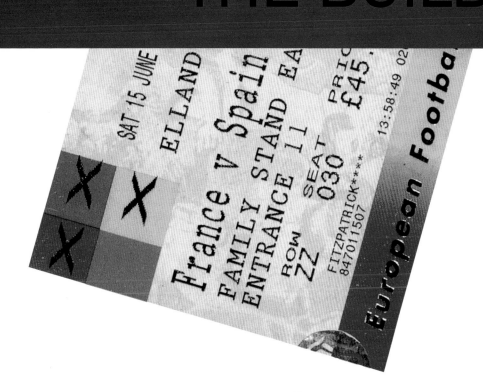

# THE BUILD UP

THE F.A. PREMIER LEAGUE

ARSENAL

BOLTON WANDERERS

CHELSEA

CRYSTAL PALACE

LEICESTER CITY

LIVERPOOL

SHEFFILED WEDNESDAY

ASTON VILLA

BARNSLEY

BLACKBURN

DERBY COUNTY

EVERTON

LEEDS UNITED

SOUTHAMPTON

TOTTENHAM HOTSPUR

WIMBLEDON

**THE FA PREMIER LEAGUE** England's top professional competition consists of 20 clubs. The selection of their badges shown here illustrates a diverse array of styles. Many of the more established clubs sport pseudo-heraldic designs that date back to their formation in the nineteenth century – with a few modern embellishments. Others, notably Barnsley with their Toby Tyke character and Sheffield Wednesday's stylised Owl (which refers to the club's nickname), take on a more modern look with echoes of corporate identity systems. Surprisingly, Arsenal and Leeds United have both recently abandoned modernist designs in favour of more traditional badges.

**MAJOR LEAGUE SOCCER** is the latest attempt to introduce football to the USA. The ten-team league was set up in 1996 with the backing of major corporations. In contrast to the organic growth of European football, each side was created from scratch by a team of marketing professionals from the league and representatives of official kit suppliers Adidas and Nike. The identities combine references and stylistic devices familiar from existing American sports, such as the dynamic names and animal characters, with modernised versions of European club badge conventions (see previous spread). A collision of visual and sporting cultures.

イラスト／那須盛之

ニアポストとボールを結んだ線上に背の高い人を置いて壁を作る

壁以外の選手はゾーンで守ってディフェンスに穴を作らゴール正面の敵からケアすること

インプレーになったら壁は"壁"のままではダメ すぐにボールへプレッシャーをかける

ストライカービデオ
②現代トッププレーヤー8

HONDA

## FKをとられたときの心得

カベを巻いて飛ぶ
強烈なシュート。G
プレーに対処しない
正しく壁を作って、

FKをとられたら、GKは即座にチームメイトへ的確な指示を送らなければならない。壁を作るのに必要な人数を呼び戻し、何人で壁を作るか、ハッキリと指示する。

また、ファウルの笛が鳴っても、すぐにシュートしてくる場合も考えて、次の笛（壁を下げるための注意など）が鳴るまでは、ボールとゴールの中心を結んだ線上にポジションを取っておく。

ペナルティエリアすぐ外のFKならば、正面で5〜7人、45度くらいの角度で3〜5人、サイドなら2、3人が壁に必要な人数の目安。

壁を作る選手は、FKの位置によってあらかじめ決めておき、試合ではそれを確認するために指示を出す。

本番で混乱しないように、あらかじめ決めた壁の作り方は、練習でも何回か予行演習しておく。

以上が基本的な守り方だが、敵の動きに応じて的確かつ迅速に味方に指示を送ることが必要だ。

例えば、キッカーが二人並んだ場合、一人がヨコにボールを流し、もう一人がシュートしてくる可能性がある。こういうときは、壁から離れた場所に味方を置き、ワンプレー後のシュートコースを防がせる。

最近では、こうしたワンプレー、ツープレー後にシュートしてくるケースが多いので、壁以外の選手の配置も穴ができないように気をつける必要がある。壁以外の選手はゾーンで守る。

巻いてクアし、流してヤ…を強っていにけない。また、壁の選手も壁のままではいけない。敵がFKを蹴ったら、ただちに壁を崩して、ボールに向かう、あるいは敵をマークするなど、次のプレーに移行する。

余談だが、よくジーコや木村（日産）のような、壁を越してカーブするFKに対して、壁が飛び上がって防ごうとする。しかし、このやり方だと万が一、低いシュートを蹴られて、飛び上がった壁の下を抜かれたら、GKはお手上げだ。

僕は、FKがプレーされるまでは壁は動かないほうがいいと思う。安全第一、あえて危険を冒すべきではない。

## ボールとニアポストを結ぶ線上が壁の起点
## 壁以外の選手はゾーンで守り、サインプレーをケア

ストライカー実戦レッスン●GK編

ボール、カベの横を抜く
……って、FKはあらゆる
……らない重要な局面だ。
……チを未然に防ごう。

**武田亘弘**（たけだのぶひろ）

1965年3月22日生まれ、大阪府出身、身長18
0cm、体重76kg、大体大卒、本田技研所属。的確
な状況判断で、好調・本田をリードするキャプテ
ン。安定したゴールキーピングに定評がある。

### 壁の作り方と
### GKのポジショニング

ニアポストとボールを結んだ線上に
起点になる選手を置き、そこからファ
ーポスト側に必要な人数を足して壁を
作る。

壁以外の選手は、ボールに近い敵か
ら順番にケアし、敵とゴールの中心を
結んだ線上に立つ。

ニアポスト側には、背の高い選手を
置いて、壁を越してくるシュートをケ
ア。

さらに、ニア側、背の高い選手の外
側にもう一人立てれば、低いカーブボ
ールが渡っても対処
できるようにする。

例えば、ゴール正面で6人の壁を作
ったとすると、GKを除いた壁以外の
選手の数は4人ということになる。
前線に一人残すとしたら、3人で守
らなければならない。敵の人数のほう
が多いのだからマンツーマンでは守れ
ない。

は、自分のゾーンに複数の敵がいると
き、最大で壁のラインまで下がってポ
ジションを取り、いちばん外の敵にボ
ールが渡っても対処できるようにする。

**THE J-LEAGUE**, Japan's first professional football league, started
up on 15 May 1993. Like Major League Soccer in the US, J-League
teams were created from scratch, with the help of Japan's biggest
advertising agency, Dentsu. In order to explain the finer points of the
game to the Japanese public, the first issue of *Striker* magazine
included a technical guide to the game, left and above, while the *Soccer
Handbook*, top, outlined who was who in the international game.

## OFFICIAL MASCOT
## VOLLEY & OVERHEAD KICK

©1995 ISL TM

| 90% Cyan<br>45% Magenta | 100% Magenta<br>90% Yellow | 15% Magenta<br>95% Yellow | 100% Black |
|---|---|---|---|
| PMS 285 C | PMS 485 C | PMS 116 C | PMS Black C |
| Black screen:<br>35% Black | Black screen:<br>70% Black | Black screen:<br>12% Black | Black screen:<br>100% Black |

© SPORT-BILLY PRODUCTIONS 1984

© 1992 WC '94 TM

FRANCE 98

© 1995 ISL TM

**MEXICO86**
© SPORT-BILLY PRODUCTIONS 1984

**ITALIA'90**
© Copyright 1986 COL ITALIA '90

**WorldCup**
**USA94**™

© 1991 WC '94/ISL   TM

FRANCE 98
WORLD CUP

© 1994 ISL TM

**TOURNAMENT LOGOS** No major football tournament is complete without a logo and a mascot with which to launch the marketing and merchandising campaigns which are central to the financial success of the modern game. Left: page from the design implementation manual for France 98's Footix mascot.

Above: mascots and logos from the four most recent World Cup finals. The mascots are, left to right, Mexico's Pique, Italy's Ciao, America's Striker and France's Footix. Below, left to right: World Cup Willie mascot from England 66, England's Euro 96 logo, logo for England's bid to host the 2006 World Cup finals.

WORLD CUP

**UEFA**
**euro 96**
*England*

© 1994 UEFA TM

**ENGLAND**
**2006**

© 1997 F.A. TM

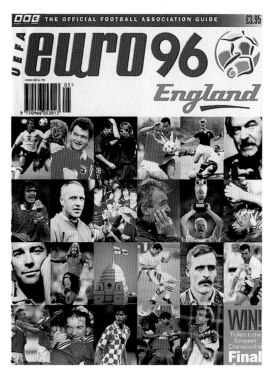

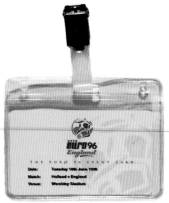

**Football Comes Home**™©

**EURO 96** was the first tournament to be hosted by England in the new commercial age of football. A thorough marketing operation was run by the FA in an attempt to ensure its success. Iconographic images of past England players and the copyline "Football Comes Home" were used to brand every aspect of the tournament, including this set of postcards, right, and the ticket envelope, above. Other printed material included the Official FA Guide (top) and hospitality passes (above). Opposite page: this press advertising campaign promoted the tournament to female fans.

FOOTBALL
COMES
HOME
Ultra 96
England

# HOW CAN I LIE BACK AND THINK OF ENGLAND WHEN VENABLES HASN'T FINALISED THE SQUAD?

EVERY FOOTBALL FAN'S DREAM COMES TRUE THIS JUNE WHEN ENGLAND HOSTS THE
1996 EUROPEAN CHAMPIONSHIP FINALS. FOR TICKETS, PHONE NOW ON 099 099 1996.

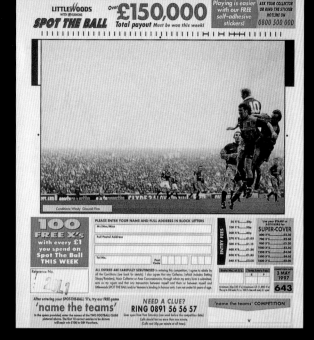

**GAMBLING** has always been a part of football – legal or otherwise. There are now numerous ways to lose your money. Above: in a classic case of appropriation, Britain's National Lottery draws on football's popularity to market a "scratchcard". Top: the British play "spot the ball" (left) while the Spanish attempt to "spot the player". Right: football pools form from Ladbrokes.

# Strike it Rich!

## SELECT ONE, TWO OR THREE RESULTS PER SECTION

**Ladbrokes**

AUG. 29/30/31/SEPT. 1 WINNINGS

£   :   p

OFFICE USE ONLY

## £1 MILLION
### CAN BE WON ON THIS COUPON

F – Playing Friday.   S – Playing Sunday.   M – Playing Monday.   ● – Live on Sky.   ■ – Live on S.T.V.

## 7 Sections List

Example winning lines for a £5 stake (deduction paid)

**1 Correct result per section wins at least £509**
**2 Correct results per section wins at least £61,136**

Mark 1 for a home win, 2 for an away win, X for a draw

| HOME | | | AWAY | | DRAW | Complete 1 or more lines | | | | |
|---|---|---|---|---|---|---|---|---|---|---|
| 4/11 | Man. Utd. | | 8/1 | Coventry | 11/4 | | | | | 9 |
| 1/2 | Chelsea | | 11/2 | Southampton | 12/5 | | | | | 5 |
| 8/13 | Sunderland | | 4/1 | Norwich | 12/5 | | | | | 20 |
| 8/13 | Livingston | | 7/2 | Qn. o'South | 5/2 | | | | | 58 |
| 4/6 | Nott'm. For. | | 10/3 | Q.P.R. | 5/2 | | | | | 16 |
| 4/6 | Portsmouth | | 7/2 | Oxford | 12/5 | | | | | 17 |
| 4/6 | Wolves | | 4/1 | Bury | 11/5 | | | | | 22 |
| 4/6 | Dundee | | 10/3 | Raith | 12/5 | | | | | 52 |
| 4/6 | Ross Co. | | 3/1 | Albion | 13/5 | | | | | 65 |
| 8/11 | Arsenal | | 7/2 | Tottenham | 11/5 | | | | | 2 |
| 8/11 | Derby | | 10/3 | Barnsley | 9/4 | | | | | 7 |
| 8/11 | Bristol C. | | 10/3 | Wigan | 9/4 | | | | | 25 |
| 8/11 | Cardiff | | 3/1 | Notts. Co. | 5/2 | | | | | 37 |
| 8/11 | Hamilton | | 11/4 | Ayr | 5/2 | | | | | 53 |
| 4/5 | Liverpool   S● | | 3/1 | Newcastle | 11/5 | | | | | 8 |
| 4/5 | Ipswich | | 11/4 | W.B.A. | 12/5 | | | | | 15 |
| 4/5 | Stoke | | 3/1 | Swindon | 9/4 | | | | | 19 |
| 4/5 | Lincoln | | 3/1 | Scarboro | 9/4 | | | | | 42 |
| 4/5 | Scunthorpe | | 11/4 | Mansfield | 12/5 | | | | | 44 |
| 4/5 | Dunfermline | | 11/4 | St. Johnstone | 12/5 | | | | | 48 |
| 4/5 | Montrose | | 5/2 | Cowdenbeath | 5/2 | | | | | 64 |
| 5/6 | Berwick | | 12/5 | Arbroath | 5/2 | | | | | 61 |
| 10/11 | Luton | | 5/2 | Oldham | 9/4 | | | | | 28 |
| 10/11 | Cambridge | | 9/4 | Shrewsbury | 5/2 | | | | | 36 |
| 10/11 | Airdrie | | 12/5 | Partick | 9/4 | | | | | 51 |
| Ev. | Aston Villa | | 9/4 | Leeds | 9/4 | | | | | 3 |
| Ev. | Burnley | | 9/4 | Bristol R. | 9/4 | | | | | 26 |
| Ev. | Carlisle | | 9/4 | Northampton | 9/4 | | | | | 27 |
| Ev. | St. Mirren | | 9/4 | Morton | 11/5 | | | | | 54 |
| Ev. | Dumbarton | | 2/1 | Alloa | 12/5 | | | | | 62 |
| 11/10 | Bolton   M● | | 2/1 | Everton | 9/4 | | | | | 4 |
| 6/5 | Sheff. Wed. | | 9/5 | Leicester | 9/4 | | | | | 10 |
| 6/5 | West Ham | | 15/8 | Wimbledon | 11/5 | | | | | 11 |
| 6/5 | Reading | | 9/5 | Bradford | 9/4 | | | | | 18 |
| 6/5 | Bournemouth | | 9/5 | Blackpool | 9/4 | | | | | 23 |
| 6/5 | Walsall | | 9/5 | Southend | 9/4 | | | | | 31 |
| 6/5 | Torquay | | 9/5 | Colchester | 9/4 | | | | | 45 |
| 6/5 | East Fife | | 7/4 | Clyde | 9/4 | | | | | 56 |
| 5/4 | Charlton | | 7/4 | Man. City | 9/4 | | | | | 12 |
| 7/4 | Huddersfield | | 5/4 | Sheff. Utd. | 9/4 | | | | | 14 |
| 5/4 | Barnet | | 7/4 | Chester | 9/4 | | | | | 34 |
| 5/4 | Brighton | | 9/5 | Leyton O. | 11/5 | | | | | 35 |
| 5/4 | Darlington | | 7/4 | Rotherham | 9/4 | | | | | 38 |
| 5/4 | Hartlepool | | 7/4 | Macclesfield | 9/4 | | | | | 40 |
| 5/4 | Rochdale | | 7/4 | Peterboro | 9/4 | | | | | 43 |
| 7/4 | Celtic   M■ | | 5/4 | Rangers | 9/4 | | | | | 47 |
| 5/4 | Stirling | | 6/4 | Falkirk | 5/2 | | | | | 55 |
| 5/4 | Stranraer | | 6/4 | Brechin | 5/2 | | | | | 60 |
| 6/4 | E. Stirling | | 5/4 | Queens Pk. | 5/2 | | | | | 63 |
| 13/8 | Stockport   F● | | 11/8 | Birmingham | 11/5 | | | | | 1 |
| 11/8 | Crewe   S● | | 8/5 | Port Vale | 11/5 | | | | | 13 |
| 11/8 | Brentford | | 13/8 | Grimsby | 11/5 | | | | | 24 |
| 11/8 | Plymouth | | 13/8 | Chesterfield | 11/5 | | | | | 29 |
| 13/8 | Wycombe | | 11/8 | Fulham | 11/5 | | | | | 32 |
| 11/8 | York | | 13/8 | Gillingham | 11/5 | | | | | 33 |
| 13/8 | Doncaster | | 11/8 | Exeter | 11/5 | | | | | 39 |
| 13/8 | Hull | | 11/8 | Swansea | 11/5 | | | | | 41 |
| 11/8 | Hibernian | | 7/4 | Hearts | 2/1 | | | | | 49 |
| 6/4 | Kilmarnock   S | | 11/8 | Motherwell | 12/5 | | | | | 50 |
| 11/8 | Forfar | | 11/8 | Clydebank | 5/2 | | | | | 57 |
| 11/8 | Stenhousemuir | | 11/8 | Inverness C.T. | 5/2 | | | | | 59 |
| 6/4 | C. Palace | | 6/4 | Blackburn | 11/5 | | | | | 6 |
| 6/4 | Tranmere | | 6/4 | Middlesbro | 11/5 | | | | | 21 |
| 6/4 | Preston | | 6/4 | Watford | 11/5 | | | | | 30 |
| 6/4 | Aberdeen | | 6/4 | Dundee Utd. | 11/5 | | | | | 46 |

**STAKE PER LINE** [ ][ ][ ][ ]

## Bonanza List

Example winning lines for a £5 stake (deduction paid)

**2 Correct results per section wins at least £19,733**
**3 Correct results per section wins £1 MILLION**

Mark 1 for a home win, 2 for an away win, X for a draw

| HOME | | | AWAY | | DRAW | Complete 1 or more lines | | | | |
|---|---|---|---|---|---|---|---|---|---|---|
| 6/5 | Sheff. Wed. | | 9/5 | Leicester | 9/4 | | | | | 10 |
| 6/5 | West Ham | | 15/8 | Wimbledon | 11/5 | | | | | 11 |
| 6/5 | Reading | | 9/5 | Bradford | 9/4 | | | | | 18 |
| 6/5 | Bournemouth | | 9/5 | Blackpool | 9/4 | | | | | 23 |
| 6/5 | Walsall | | 9/5 | Southend | 9/4 | | | | | 31 |
| 6/5 | Torquay | | 9/5 | Colchester | 9/4 | | | | | 45 |
| 5/4 | Charlton | | 7/4 | Man. City | 9/4 | | | | | 12 |
| 7/4 | Huddersfield | | 5/4 | Sheff. Utd. | 9/4 | | | | | 14 |
| 5/4 | Barnet | | 7/4 | Chester | 9/4 | | | | | 34 |
| 5/4 | Brighton | | 9/5 | Leyton O. | 11/5 | | | | | 35 |
| 5/4 | Darlington | | 7/4 | Rotherham | 9/4 | | | | | 38 |
| 5/4 | Hartlepool | | 7/4 | Macclesfield | 9/4 | | | | | 40 |
| 13/8 | Stockport   F● | | 11/8 | Birmingham | 11/5 | | | | | 1 |
| 11/8 | Crewe   S● | | 8/5 | Port Vale | 11/5 | | | | | 13 |
| 11/8 | Brentford | | 13/8 | Grimsby | 11/5 | | | | | 24 |
| 11/8 | Plymouth | | 13/8 | Chesterfield | 11/5 | | | | | 29 |
| 7/4 | Celtic   M■ | | 5/4 | Rangers | 9/4 | | | | | 47 |
| 5/4 | Stirling | | 6/4 | Falkirk | 5/2 | | | | | 55 |
| 13/8 | Wycombe | | 11/8 | Fulham | 11/5 | | | | | 32 |
| 11/8 | York | | 13/8 | Gillingham | 11/5 | | | | | 33 |
| 13/8 | Doncaster | | 11/8 | Exeter | 11/5 | | | | | 39 |
| 13/8 | Hull | | 11/8 | Swansea | 11/5 | | | | | 41 |
| 11/8 | Hibernian | | 7/4 | Hearts | 2/1 | | | | | 49 |
| 6/4 | Kilmarnock   S | | 11/8 | Motherwell | 12/5 | | | | | 50 |
| 6/4 | C. Palace | | 6/4 | Blackburn | 11/5 | | | | | 6 |
| 6/4 | Tranmere | | 6/4 | Middlesbro | 11/5 | | | | | 21 |
| 6/4 | Preston | | 6/4 | Watford | 11/5 | | | | | 30 |
| 6/4 | Aberdeen | | 6/4 | Dundee Utd. | 11/5 | | | | | 46 |
| 11/8 | Forfar | | 11/8 | Clydebank | 5/2 | | | | | 57 |
| 11/8 | Stenhousemuir | | 11/8 | Inverness C.T. | 5/2 | | | | | 59 |

**STAKE PER LINE** [ ][ ][ ][ ]

Minimum total stake on this coupon is 50p. All prices subject to fluctuation.
All bets subject to Ladbrokes Football Rules.
Maximum number of draws in any one line = 5.

**REMEMBER – ALL SELECTIONS MUST BE CORRECT TO WIN**
IF YOU NEED ANY ASSISTANCE PLEASE ASK OUR STAFF

**PICK UP YOUR WINNINGS ON SATURDAY AFTER THE FINAL WHISTLE!**

### SEE REVERSE FOR LEAGUE TABLES & FORM GUIDE

| STAKE FOR ALL BETS | £ | : | p |
|---|---|---|---|
| DEDUCTION PAID | £ | : | p |
| TOTAL STAKE | £ | : | p |

CODE: C3

**PRODUCTS** aimed at a young market often seek to link themselves to the popularity of football by borrowing its imagery. In Britain, this has been a fairly recent phenomenon due largely to the relative decline of hooliganism. Featured: Chee-tos from Portugal and, from Britain, Gary Lineker-endorsed crisps and a Premier League-endorsed cereal.

FOOTY LUCKY BAG

COLLECTOR CARDS

STICKERS

SWEETS & SURPRISES

FOOTY FAN

INCLUDES AUTOGRAPH COLLECTOR CARDS

Arsenal

The Carousel Company ™

For reference - Not Suitable for children under 36 months,- Adult supervision recommended
May contain a small toy or novelty not edible - contents may be the product of more than one country.

CONTENTS OF THE CONFECTIONARY WILL VARY AND MAY CONTAIN THE FOLLOWING INGREDIENTS:
Sugar, modified starch, gelatin, citric acid, anticaking agent, magnesium stearate, glucose syrup,
corn crisp, gelatine, malic acid, dextrose, E834, E400, flavours, colour, E102, E110, E120, E122, E124, E132,
E133, E131, E142, E150, E153, E160B, E270, glazing, beeswax, E330, E104, E572, E296, lactic acid.

**ALCOHOL** may have been the cause of some of football's greatest problems both on and off the pitch but that has not stopped brewers becoming heavily involved in the game. Here, Carling links its packaging to its sponsorship of the English Premier League and Sagres boasts of its backing for the Portuguese national team.

**MERCHANDISING** for football clubs has exploded in recent years. The true fans, it seems, must assert their loyalty over everything they own, whether that be their clothing, in their home or in their car. Some of the largest clubs now generate over half their income from sales of endorsed products. Clockwise from top: Bayern Munich felt hat; Real Madrid car freshener; Benfica wall pennant; Real Madrid pillow which plays the club song; Del Piero statuette; Paris St Germain shower gel; St Etienne keyring; Alan Shearer inflatable doll; David Seaman phone card; Juventus sew-on badge.

Opposite page: Manchester United wallpaper.

PINTO
J. COSTA
F.C.PORTO
S. CONCEIÇÃO
F.C.PORTO
P. SA

RONALDO

12548

Viva el Barça

F.C.B.

**TOS**
F.C.PORTO

**ARTUR**

**DOMINGOS**
F.C.PORTO

**JARDEL**

**STICKER COLLECTIONS** are a major business across Europe. In Spain, England and France fans can collect their favourite stars and keep them in a special annual. In Portugal stickers come free with packs of bubble gum (bottom right).

Above: FC Porto scarf from Portugal. Left: Barcelona briefs strengthen fans' support.

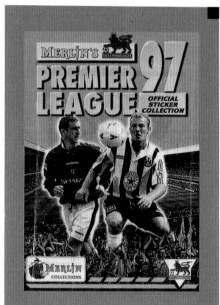

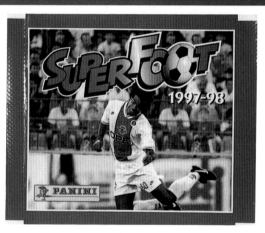

JULIO CESAR

REAL VALLADOLID

RUUD GULLIT

Laurent BLANC

YOURI DJORKAEFF
FRANÇA
338

LYON, 9-3-1968
1,79 m. 72 kg.
INTER MILAN, AVANÇADO

**FRANCE 98** is the biggest World Cup finals yet in terms of sponsorship and merchandising. The mascot, Footix, was designed by Dragon Rouge following a nationwide competition. The cuddly cockerel is a fresh take on France's national sporting symbol. His image appears on official merchandise, including the coasters, plates,

clothing, fridge magnets and soft toys shown. In addition, his use has been licensed to multinational sponsors, including Fuji (disposable camera shown left).
Left: La Poste has produced a set of stamps to commemorate the tournament, with a separate design for each venue.

**CAR WINDOWS** have become a customary place for fans to display loyalties. Pendants, mini-strips and decals are all used, often carrying a "witty" message. Such displays can border on the reckless if the owners leave their cars in a rival team's neighbourhood. Taking things a step further is a sponsored London taxi pictured during Euro 96.

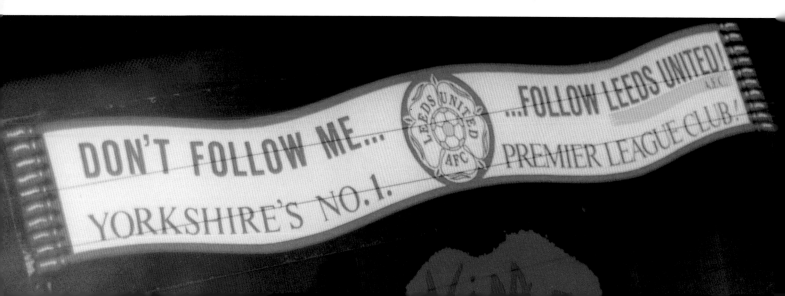

# The Football Association Challenge Cup

SPONSORED BY

F.A. CUP SPONSOR **LITTLEWOODS**

SATURDAY 17TH
MAY 1997

FINAL TIE

THE CUP FINAL TIE 1997

| BLOCK | ROW | | CHELSEA F.C. | | | | KICK OFF 3.00PM - TURNSTILES 1.00PM |
|---|---|---|---|---|---|---|---|
| 228 | 15 | TO BE GIVEN UP | TURNSTILE L | | | | PLEASE TAKE YOUR SEATS BY 2.15PM |

BLOCK     ROW     SEAT

228   15   128                    £60.00

SEAT
128

£60.00          6     869  010597  141323A

*Wembley*

TO BE RETAINED

ESTADI
F.C. BARCELONA

N.I.F. G.08-26629-8          I.V.A. INCLOS

CAMPIONAT NACIONAL LLIGA 1.DIVISIO-22.JORNADA

CLUB ATLETICO DE MADRID - F.C.BARCELONA
TRIBUNA SEGONA GRADERIA

PORTA - 3          FILA - 30

BOCA - 300          NUM. - 3     101

**TICKETS** send out a complex combination of visual messages. They must combine the traditional stylings of banknotes, to imply a heightened sense of worth and as a signifier of their being genuine, with the commercial realities of the modern game – sponsors' logos and the need to present the game as a modern, dynamic product. Also, as with banknotes, forgery is a major problem so that protective devices must be incorporated into the design, including holograms and metallic inks. Those not lucky enough to get hold of a ticket can still enjoy the big match atmosphere by watching the game on television in their local bar or pub, as advertised on this blackboard (facing page).

SAT 22 JUNE 1996  15:00

# WEMBLEY STADIUM

# Quarter Final
## SOUTH TERRACE
## TURNSTILE M

| BLOCK | ROW | SEAT | PRICE |
|-------|-----|------|-------|
| 125 | 7 | 40 | £35.00 |

JEFFERSON
028855401

ADVERT BOARD RESTRICTS VIEW
15:04:38 120496 SYNCHRO

# European Football Championship 1996

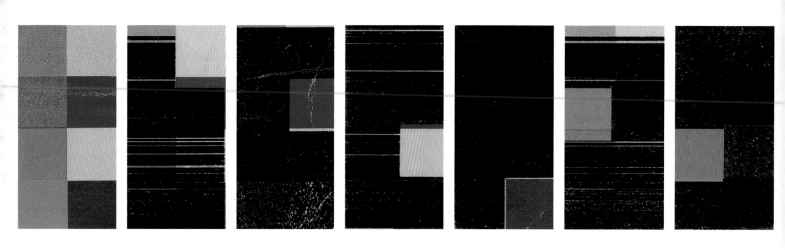

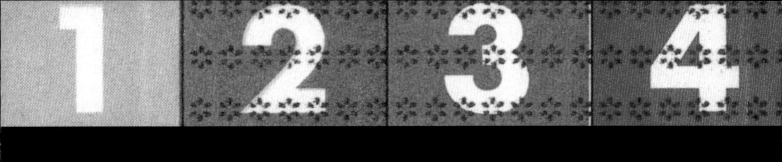

Throughout the world, the visual language of football provides familiar reference points, as shown here by tickets from three different countries. On the bottom left are details from a series of tickets to Chelsea games featuring the club's colour-coded guide to the seats' location within the stadium. A similar device was used during Euro 96 (top left) and Italia 90 (top). Shown left is a ticket to an England international from 1981 – an era before commercialism forced football to update its image.

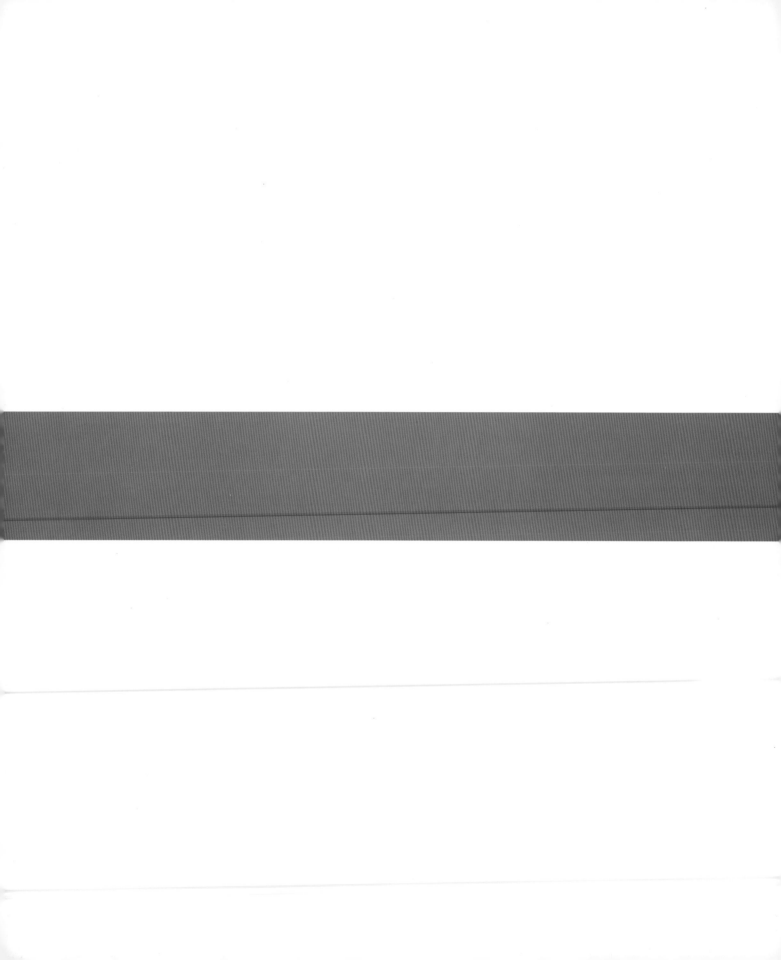

# THE GAME

**FACE PAINTING** has become the norm among committed fans attending matches. The fans shown above were photographed by Stuart Clarke during Euro 96 and are supporters of (clockwise from top left): Italy; Turkey; Scotland, and England. Right: a Middlesbrough fan pictured shortly before his team played Chelsea in the 1997 English FA Cup final. They lost.

**FANS** provide the true colour and atmosphere at a football match, not cheerleaders or mascots. Left: AC Milan supporters at the San Siro stadium provide the traditional welcome for their heroes. In Italy, fan clubs spend huge amounts of time and money bidding to outdo each other with their banners and complex displays of loyalty. Below left: fans show support on a smaller scale, spelling out their hero's name on their heads. This page: the team shirt has largely replaced the scarf as badge of loyalty in the nineties. Left to right, from top: Austria Memphis; Juventus; France; Arsenal; Portsmouth; Spurs; Ajax; Wimbledon; Newcastle; Manchester United; Italy; Chelsea.

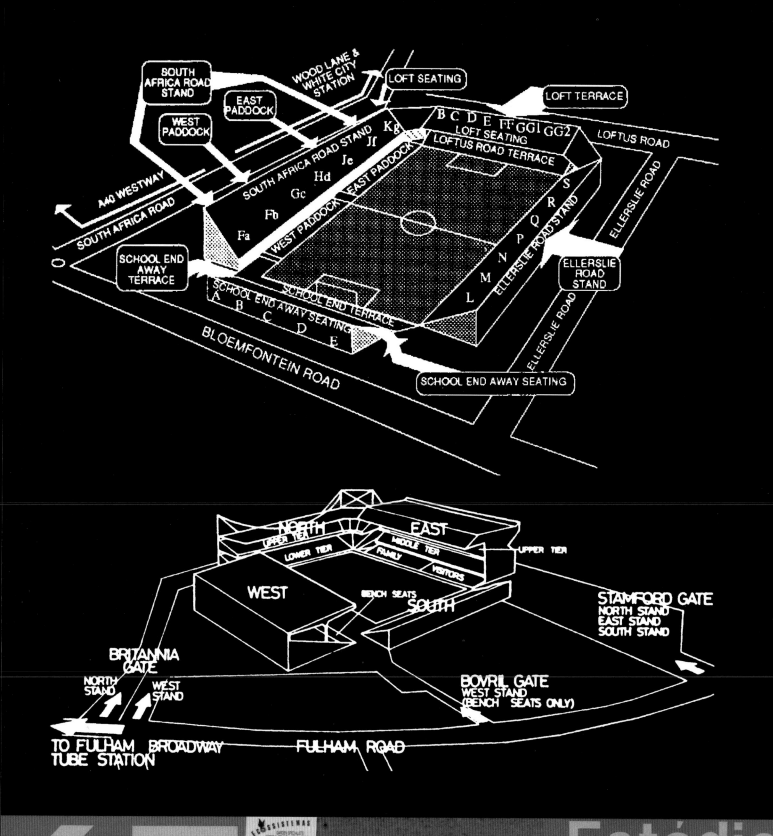

Estádio
Municipal

**STADIA** offer a major challenge to the designer. Information must be clearly conveyed while conforming to the stylistic traditions of the game. Clockwise from top right: main stand at Deepdale, Preston North End, featuring portrait of legendary player Tom Finney; seat markings at the Olympic Stadium, Rome; signage at Wembley Stadium; road sign, Portugal; back of ticket for Chelsea, London; back of ticket for Queen's Park Rangers, London, the last two showing schematic diagrams of the stadia, entrances and surrounding streets.

# liverpoo

# UNITED

# SKY BLUE

# CHAMPION LEEDS

# VISITING CAPTAIN

# TODAY'S REFEREE

# COMING UP

# HALF TIMES

# MISTER MAGIC

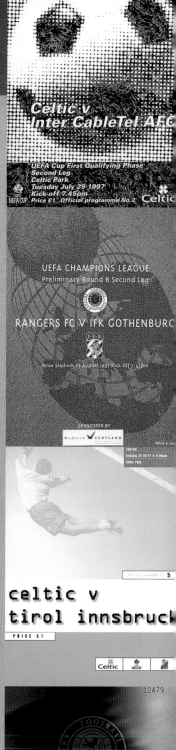

**MATCH PROGRAMMES** are highly collectable items, yet few feature designs of any merit – these classics from the seventies prove this was not always so. Glasgow Development Agency has tried to reacquaint programmes with good design by inviting local studios to create covers for Rangers' and Celtic's 97/98 European games, right.

# SKY BLUE

SKY BLUE, THE OFFICIAL MAGAZINE OF THE COVENTRY CITY FOOTBALL CLUB LIMITED/VOLUME ONE/NUMBER FIFTEEN

Your 'Sky Blue' host for today's Football League Division One game is Jeff Blockley. The match: **Sky Blues v Stoke City.** The place: Highfield Road. The date: 5th December 1970. Kick-off: 3.15 pm. Goalkeeper Gordon Banks, captain of today's visitors in the absence of the injured Peter Dobing, brings to Highfield Road a Stoke side including some of the games most promising youngsters, Denis Smith, Terry Conroy, Mike Bernard and John Mahoney! In today's magazine: Stoke, Focus on Jeff Blockley, Saturday Men and Junior Sky Blues.

PRESIDENT Dr CUTHBERT K. N. BARDSLEY, C.B.E., M.A. (LORD BISHOP OF COVENTRY). CHAIRMAN DERRICK H. ROBINS VICE-CHAIRMAN J. R. MEAD, J.P., F.C.A. DIRECTORS PETER D. H. ROBINS, MICHAEL FRENCH, F.C.A., THOMAS SERGEANT, F.R.C.S MEDICAL OFFICER Dr T. BAIRD. GENERAL MANAGER NOEL CANTWELL. SECRETARY EDDIE PLUMLEY, CHEF & CATERING MANAGER FRANK HUNT. MAITRE d'HOTEL GIOVANNI. ADVERTISING CONSULTANT PETER STURTZ. MAGAZINE EDITOR JOHN ELVIN

COVENTRY CITY v STOKE CITY/5th DECEMBER 1970/'SKY BLUE' OFFICIAL MATCHDAY MAGAZINE  (10 N.P.)

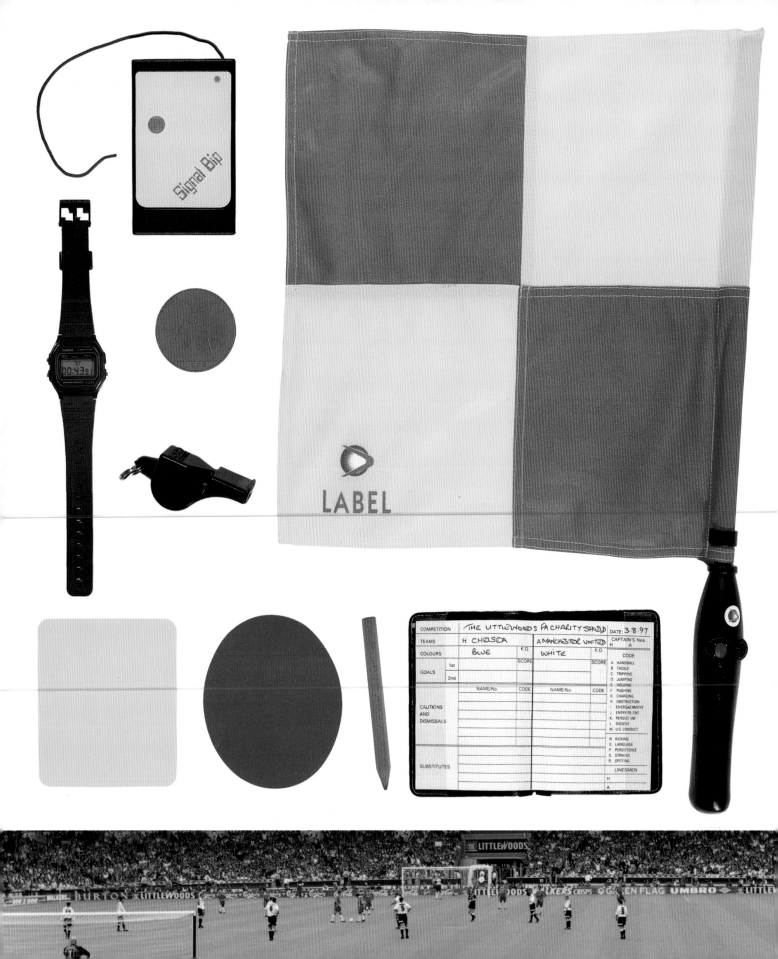

# 90 minutes of agonising, gut wrenching tension. Can't wait.

UMBRO®
Only Football

**REFEREES** are responsible for controlling and timing matches. The equipment shown opposite was photographed before being used by referee Peter Jones during the 1997 Charity Shield match between Manchester United and Chelsea played at Wembley Stadium, pictured botttom left. The assistants' flags (one shown) now have a button that triggers a buzzer (top left) worn by the referee. To avoid mistakes, the red and yellow cards are not only different shapes but are kept by the referee in different pockets of his shirt. Jones always carries an old Penny to determine which team kicks off.

Football is our **religion**

We know how you feel. We feel the same way.

SKY

Vivez Football.
Vibrez Football.
Buvez Coca-Cola.

Coca-Cola

## One *day you will see a goal*
# so beautiful
### you will want to marry it, have children and move to a small tropical island.

*Eat Football. Sleep Football. Drink Coca-Cola.*

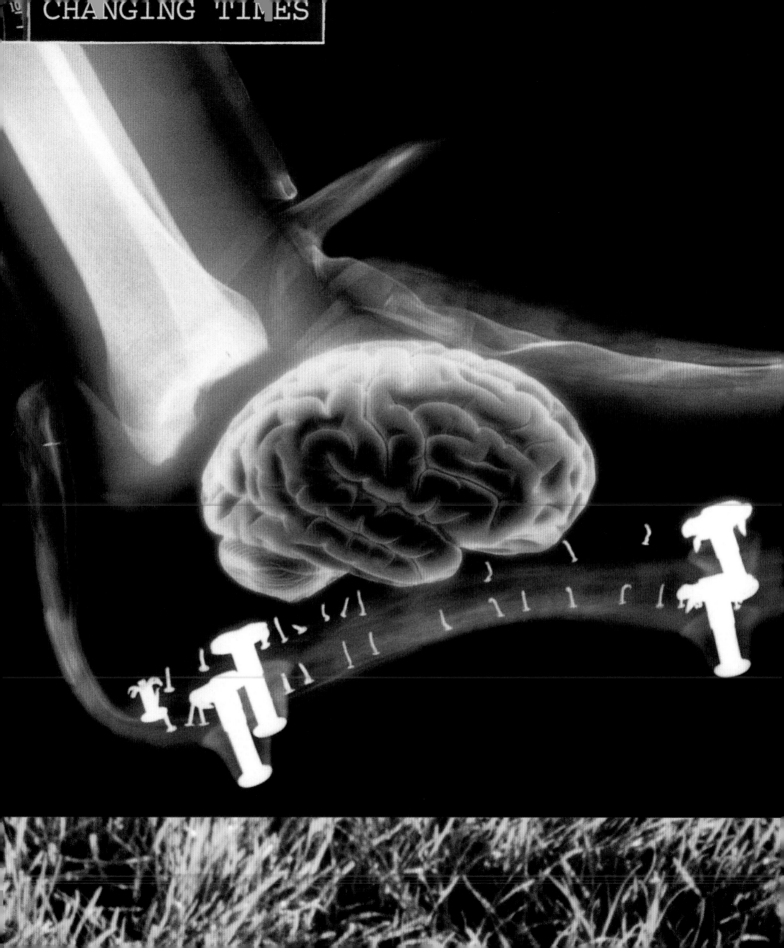

THE ✦ TIMES
Under the skin of sport

No opposition

Serious Bier

**THE MARKINGS** on a football pitch create an unmistakable graphic device, although the designer of this ad for Beck's beer (left) appears to have forgotten to include the "D" on the edge of the penalty area. Pictured above is the penalty box of Newcastle United's St James' Park, photographed by Julian Germain for a 1996 booklet of similar close-up shots entitled *Holy Grounds*.

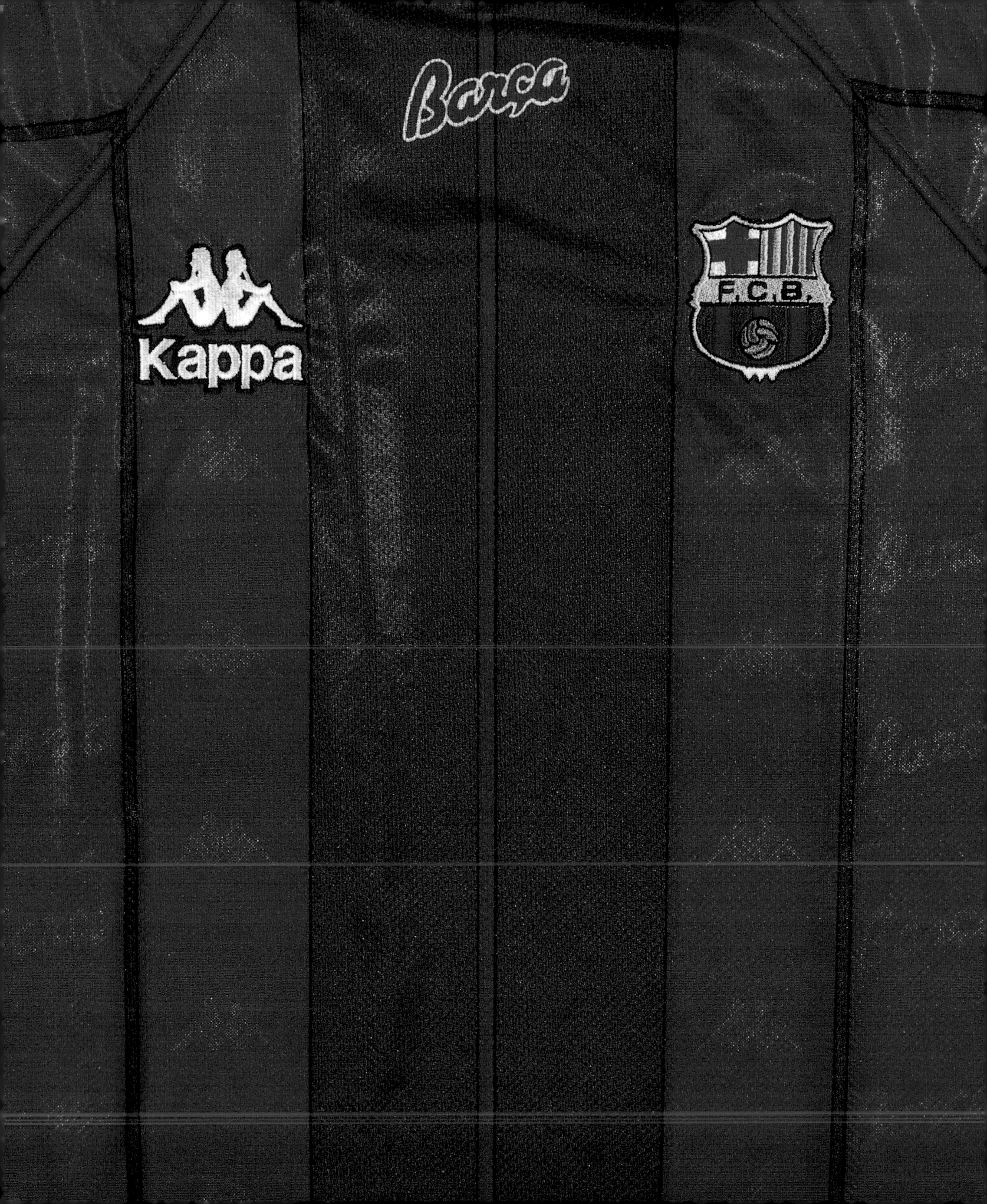
Barça
Kappa
F.C.B.

**CLUB SPONSORS'** logos have become a part of the teams' visual identity. Most visible on players' shirts, but also plastered all over stadia, match programmes and any other associated material, a sponsor can become inextricably linked with a particular team – great if the team is winning, not so good if it gets relegated. Shown on this page are details of shirts of (left to right, from top): Juventus; Manchester United; PSV Eindhoven; Glasgow Rangers; Liverpool; Munich 1860; Bayern Munich; FC Cologne and AC Milan. Barcelona (opposite page) is almost unique in the professional game for not allowing its famous shirt to be sullied by a sponsor's logo.

NECAXA, MEXICO

INTER MILAN, ITALY

PENAROL, URUGUAY

FLAMENCO, BRAZIL

UNITED STATES

CROATIA

ITALY

NIGERIA

HOLLAND

AJAX, HOLLAND

PSV EINDHOVEN, HOLLAND

MUNICH 1860, GERMANY

NORWAY

NORGE

WOVEN TAB
S.S.LAZIO

BACK NECK DETAIL

LAZIO, ITALY

CIRIO

VAPA TECH TAB
VAPA
TECH

ENGLAND (AWAY)

UMBRO

ENGLAND

MANCHESTER UNITED, ENGLAND
(GOALKEEPER)

UMBRO

SHARP

MANCHESTER UNITED
F.C

AJAX, HOLLAND (AWAY)

UMBRO

ABN·AMRO

A.F.C.
AJAX

INTER MILAN, ITALY (GOALKEEPER)

PIRELLI

**FASHION** has frequently borrowed stylings from football but never as explicitly as in this range of t-shirts designed by Paul Smith for his R. Newbold range in 1997, above. Left and below: kit designs are now developed in the same manner as fashion lines. Umbro uses these CAD sketches to create its styles and to use in the design approval process.

BACK VIEW

ENGLAND (GOALKEEPER)

VAPA TECH TAB

VAPA
TECH *PERFORMANCE*

| STYLE CONFIRMED UMBRO | STYLE CONFIRMED A NOTHER |
|---|---|
|  |  |
| DATE | DATE |

**STRIP MANUFACTURERS** A major tournament is a huge marketing exercise for a company such as Adidas or Nike. Companies will bring out new designs especially for the occasion – sometimes the same design will be worn by several of the company's sponsored teams with colour changes appropriate to each country. Success for their team on the field is vital for a manufacturer as no-one wants to be associated with losers. Opposite: line up for Adidas (left to right) Jürgen Klinsmann, Germany; Didier Deschamps, France; Diego Simeone, Barcelona. Above: for Nike, Celestine Babayaro, Nigeria; Roberto Carlos, Brazil; Dennis Bergkamp, Holland.

**STARS** are in constant demand to promote the products of sponsors who, in turn, attempt to portray their players as ever more powerful and dynamic. Shown above: two of a series of Nike ads which turned Dutch players into computer games characters, thus linking their customers' favourite pastimes. Below: Adidas stars, including Paul Ince and Matthias Sammer, battle their clones. Right: an animated Ryan Giggs for Reebok.

**NIKE ADVERTISING** has consistently attempted to speak to fans on an emotional level about their sport. In football it has addressed the parallels between sport and conflict (in *Good Versus Evil*, below, Nike's players beat a team of demons), the fear inspired by great players (below right) and the fantasy of having a star play for your Sunday side.

IF THE DEFENSE COULD USE THEIR HANDS, THEY'D PRAY.

Just Do It

ROMA

COPPA DEL MONDO FIFA
ITALIA '90

REP. IRLANDA 0
ITALIA 1

Marcatore: 38' SCHILLACI

EAT FOOTBALL

SLEEP FOOTBALL

DRINK COCA-COLA

HEAD TO HEAD

| 150 | GAMES | 150 |
| 56 | WON | 61 |
| 33 | DRAWN | 33 |
| 223 | GOALS | 231 |

CITROËN

Coca-Cola

**SCOREBOARDS** which can also replay goals and run animated sequences are becoming common. Shown above and far left is the state-of-the-art video screen at Arsenal's Highbury Stadium. Earlier models, such as at Rome's Stadio Olympico pictured, top left, during the 1990 World Cup, merely displayed the score. Near left: a Coke ad picks up on the graphic style made familiar by early scoreboards.

Away from the razzmatazz of the professional game, even the most basic football match can provide a powerful emotional pull. This Nadav Kander photograph of an impromptu game in a South African township was used for an Umbro advertising campaign.

# THE AFTERMATH

**TELEVISION** provides money which is vital to the prosperity of football and, in turn, football provides the mass audiences vital to the success of television stations: securing the rights to Premiership games was a vital factor in the growth of satellite broadcaster BSkyB. Watching the game on television, viewers are bombarded with commercial messages and informational graphics. Shown above is the title sequence for the BBC's Match of the Day highlights programme, and above that the titles for its Euro 96 coverage. Below: titles for Sky Sports' Super Sunday coverage. Right: perimeter advertising hoardings have become as much a part of the visual experience of watching a professional football match as the pitch markings and the goalposts. This prime advertising opportunity occurred during Euro 96.

## MONDAY NIGHT FOOTBALL

► BLACKBURN ROVERS

VERSUS

► SHEFFIELD WED

FROM EWOOD PARK

CARLING

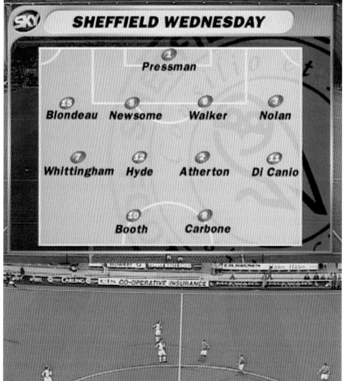

## SHEFFIELD WEDNESDAY

Pressman

Blondeau  Newsome  Walker  Nolan

Whittingham  Hyde  Atherton  Di Canio

Booth  Carbone

### BLACKBURN v SHEFF WED
Exclusively Live from Ewood Park

## MATCH FACTS

### 1ST HALF ACTION AREAS

BLACKBURN | 11% | 66% | 23% | SHEFF WED

TIME 47:56  BALL IN PLAY 29:01

Blackburn  50%–50%  Sheff Wed

B'BURN 1
SHEFF W 0
5:41

| 12 | Graham **HYDE** | Sheff Wed |
| --- | --- | --- |
| | BOOKED | |

### HOW THEY STAND  CARLING

| TOP | | PLD | PTS |
| --- | --- | --- | --- |
| ► 1 | Blackburn Rovers | 4 | 10 |
| ▲ 2 | Arsenal | 3 | 7 |
| ▼ 3 | Manchester United | 3 | 7 |
| ► 4 | Leicester City | 3 | 7 |
| ▲ 5 | Crystal Palace | 3 | 6 |
| ▲ 6 | Newcastle United | 2 | 6 |
| ▼ 7 | West Ham United | 3 | 6 |
| ► 8 | Bolton Wanderers | 2 | 4 |
| ▼ 9 | Leeds United | 3 | 4 |
| ▲ 10 | Coventry City | 3 | 4 |

**SKY SPORTS** claims that its subscription-based coverage of the British game has revolutionised football broadcasting. Innovations available to presenter Andy Gray (far left, top) include the Telestrator (far left, middle and bottom) which plots the path of shots on goal and measures their speed. Football computer games are among the most successful on the market (see p82), but in an intriguing turnaround, Sky has borrowed from computer games' graphic stylings in its Virtual Replay System (left), where goals and controversial incidents are analysed after the game using digital reconstructions, and in its informational displays (this page).

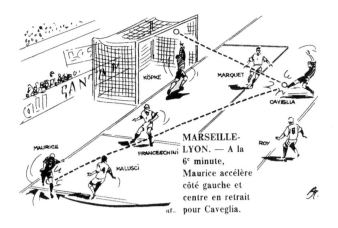

MARSEILLE-LYON. — A la 6ᵉ minute, Maurice accélère côté gauche et centre en retrait pour Caveglia.

**MAGAZINES** provide fans with in-depth analysis of the game and all the background on their heroes. As well as general football titles, there has been a huge growth in contract magazines dealing specifically with one club. Inter and AC Milan, Liverpool, Barcelona and Chelsea are just some of the big clubs to pull in extra revenues via a dedicated

magazine. Manchester United Magazine sells over 116,000 copies worldwide.

Top: some examples of analysis graphics used in football magazines. From left to right: graphics from *France Football*, *Gazzetta dello Sport* (Italy), *The Guardian* (UK), *Jogo* (Portugal) and *Fast Touch* (Hong Kong).

**COMPUTER GAMES** allow the armchair fan to pit digitised versions of real players against each other in their own homes. State-of-the-art Actua Soccer 2 from Gremlin Interactive, shown, features 64 current international teams with the correct strips and the correct line-ups. Created with the help of Alan Shearer, the commentary is by BBC TV's Barry Davies and ex-England international Trevor Brooking and the referee is a digitised version of Keith Hackett, a top English official.
Below: some fans prefer a more old-fashioned form of football simulation. Table football bars are extremely popular in France and Spain, often boasting organised leagues.
Far left: this Pocket Football game gives the lone player the chance to simulate a game in the palm of his or her hand.

**ART's** desire to tap into, examine and reinterpret popular culture has made football a primary target. The exhibits shown are from *Offside!* – an English touring exhibition of football art, with work from 13 artists from Argentina, Britain, Columbia and Mexico. Facing page, top: *Pasión de Multitudes* by Rosana Fuertes, a series of imaginary football shirt designs which include political and personal allusions. Bottom: Adam Beebee's *Ultras*, inspired by the banners of Italian fans. This page, above: *Bet I Finish My Sticker Book Before You* by Natalie Turner. Below: *Stud* by Freddy Contreras – Vivienne Westwood shoes fitted with football studs.

118 TRACKS FEATURIN...

...ER UNITED CAL...

...HAM HOTSPUR *

how to resist?

...LÉ * I LOVE GEO...

bend it! gr...

FIELDS * STA...

fantasy. romance. flair. football...

...MATTHEWS * LIVERPOOL'S KOP O...

KEVIN KEEGAN

georgie

RYAN GIGGS

LEEDS UNITED

GEORGE * ERIC...

the Best album

HOME * CRUYFF * BECKENBA...

MARADONA * BOBBY MOORE...

bend it!
1992

soccer-boppers...

exotica presents...   football à la carte

pop explosion... football-style...

bend it! 95

bend it! gr...

the flying soccer...

Three Lions  Baddiel & Skinner & LightningSeeds
The official song of the England football team

663273 2

**MUSIC** has frequently glorified star players and expressed fans' love of the game. The *bend it!* series (left) includes many of the finest, and more idiosyncratic, examples of football-related songs from around the world. It has become common practice for sides to release a team record before the start of a major tournament or a cup final. One of the most successful was England's Euro 96 release *Three Lions* which topped the UK charts for several weeks. The cover, above, uses the badge which appears on the England players' shirts.

The 1970 England Football Squad

"The World Beaters Sing The World Beaters"

Follow the Winning
Team through to the Final

Mexico '70 World Cup Final

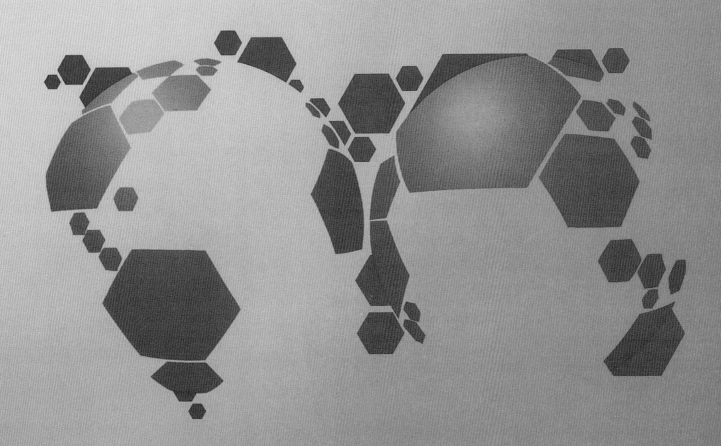

# ENGLANDneworder
## world in motion...

Left: the 1970 souvenir record by the England World Cup squad *The World Beaters Sing The World Beaters* includes such timeless classics as *Sugar, Sugar, Puppet On A String* and *There'll Always Be An England*, as well as the first England World Cup team song *Back Home*. The art-work celebrates England's only World Cup success in 1966.

Above: a team song of a more recent vintage. The England squad team up with New Order and comic actor Keith Allen before Italia 90 on *World In Motion* – musically the best effort so far. Cover by Peter Saville.

Verdy official Homepage!

Verdy News

97熱闘Verdy

Verdy プロフィール

Verdy 公式戦記録

チケット情報

ホーム スタジアム

ファンクラブ &サポーター

グッズ& ショップ

ユースチーム& スクール情報

Verdy Links

**THE INTERNET** is now home to thousands of football websites. Just about every team in the world has a presence – both through official web pages and via sites set up by enthusiastic fans. The visual language of the game is extended into the new media using iconographic balls and club badges while team colours are carried through as branding devices and simple graphic backgrounds. Opposite: English newspaper *The Guardian* has one of the best of a growing number of online football services. Over page: France 98 website

**NEWSDESK
THE GOALS**

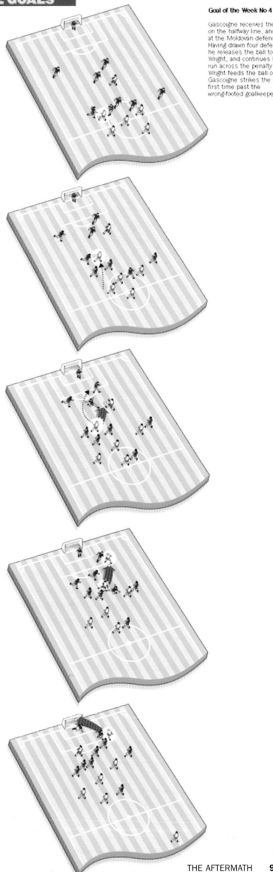

**Goal of the Week No 4**

Gascoigne receives the ball on the halfway line, and runs at the Moldovan defence. Having drawn four defenders, he releases the ball to Ian Wright, and continues his run across the penalty area. Wright feeds the ball on, and Gascoigne strikes the ball first time past the wrong-footed goalkeeper.

**Design by Jeremy Leslie**
**Text by Patrick Burgoyne**

*For Cameron*

**Special thanks**
Jamie Camplin, Peter Jones, Colin
Gooch at Soccerscene, Jim Phelan,
Paul Fuller and Mark Hyde at BSkyB,
Steve Aspinall at BBC Sport, Chas
Sharp at ISL Marketing, Richard Dean,
Arthur Smith, Glen Littlewood at
Umbro, Ken Ridden, Ken Wilcox,
Hazel Rosco, Mike Inman, Helen Willis,
Miles Pearce, Tom Engel, Stuart Clarke,
Grant McDougall, John Gill, Natalie
Turner, Rosana Fuertes, Sarah
Lockwood, Lee Cable, Graham
Mackrell, Phil Alexander, Andrew
Watson, Paul Mace, David Barnard,
Paul Hazelby, Clare Tomlinson, MJ
Spinks, Joanna McCominsky, Simon
Marland, Jim Fearn, Lynne Sympson,
Brian Truscott, Ian Cotton, John
Ireland, Abdul Rashid, Nick Moyle,
Dean Fitzpatrick, Lesley Allan,
Christophe Gowans, Lewis Blackwell,
Laurence King

Thank you to Eurostar for transport
to France

**Credits**
Still life photography by Richard Dean
**Front cover** Main photograph by Julian
Germain; Top row, left to right: detail
from Real Madrid car freshener (p28);
Juventus team strip (p60); detail from
Italia 90 logo (p19); sign advertising TV
coverage of match (p36). Bottom row:
detail of match ticket (p37); detail from
Sagres beer can (p27); *el Gol* magazine
masthead (p79); detail from England
2000 World Cup Campaign (p21)

**p4** Nike ad by Me Company for
Wieden & Kennedy, Amsterdam
**9** *Fever Pitch* poster designed by
David Groves
**12/13** Courtesy of the clubs
**14/15** Courtesy of MLS Marketing
**16/17** Lent by Jim Phelan
**18/19** World Cup logos and mascots
courtesy of ISL Marketing. Euro 96 logo
designed by MCW. England 2000 logo
designed by Real Time Studios
**20** Euro 96 promotional items designed

by MCW. Official FA Guide cover
designed by Alex Evans
**21** Euro 96 advertising by McCann-
Erickson: copywriter, Chris
Aldhous; art director, Peter Hodgson;
photographer, Peter Storey
**42** Photographs by Stuart Clarke
**43** Photograph by Jeremy Leslie
**44** Photograph by Tony
Edenden/Sportsphoto
**45** Photographs by Jeremy Leslie
and Patrick Burgoyne
**47** Preston North End Deepdale
stadium designed by Ben Casey
at The Chase
**48/49** Coventry programmes designed
by Sportsgraphic.
**49** Scottish programmes designed by:
Tank (Celtic v Intercable); Pointsize
(Rangers v IFK Gothenberg); 999
Design (Celtic v Tirrol Innsbruck);
Quorum (Rangers v Gotu Itrottarfelag)
**51** Umbro ad by DMB&B: copywriter,
Nick Hastings; art director, David
Godfree. Reebok 1997 Liverpool away
kit ad by Lowe Howard-Spink: copywriter, Paul Silburn; art director, Simon
Morris; photographer, Rory Carnegie

**52/53** Coca Cola campaign by Wieden
& Kennedy, Amsterdam: creative
directors, Bob Moore and Michael
Prieve; copywriter, Jon Matthews; art
director, Ollie Watson; photographers,
Sam Bayer and Niels van Iperen
**54/55** *The Times* ad by Rainey Kelly
Campbell Roalfe: copywriter, Phil
Cockrell; art director, Graham Storey;
photographer, Tim O'Sullivan; image
manipulation, John Whillock
**56** Beck's ad by Mountain View/Barker
& Ralston: copywriter, Richard Carman;
art director, Julian Scott
**57** Photograph by Julian Germain from
*Holy Grounds* with KesselsKramer
**59/61** Shirts lent by Soccerscene,
Carnaby Street, London W1
**62/3** Illustrations supplied by Umbro
**63** Shirts by Paul Smith
**64/65** Photographs by All Sports
**66** Nike ads by Me Company for
Wieden & Kennedy, Amsterdam. Adidas
Predator Traxion *The Difference*
commercial by Leagas Delaney:
copywriter, Rob Burleigh; art director,
Dave Beverley; director, Mehdi
Norowzian of Joy Films

# ACKNOWLEDGEMENTS

**67** Reebok Doppelganger commercial by Lowe Howard-Spink: copywriter, Paul Silburn; art director, Vince Squibb; production company, Passion Pictures; director, Nick Donkin; production designer, Deane Taylor; executive producer, Andrew Ruhemann; producer, Hugo Sands

**68** Nike *Good v Evil* commercial by Wieden & Kennedy, Amsterdam: written by Glenn Cole and David "Jelly" Helm; directed by Tarsem. Nike *Parklife* commercial by TBWA Simons Palmer: copywriter, Tony Malcolm; art director, Guy Moore; director, Jonathan Glazer; production company, Academy. Romario ad by Wieden & Kennedy, Amsterdam: creative directors, Michael Prieve and Bob Moore; copywriter, Ernest Lupinacci; art director, Michael Prieve; portrait photograph, Norbert Schroner; product shot, Hans Pieterse.

**70** Photograph of Arsenal big screen courtesy of ScreenCo

**71** Photograph by Coloursport

**72/3** Photograph by Nadav Kander

**76** BBC TV Euro 96 and Match of the Day titles designed by Steve Aspinall and Laurence Henry. Sky Super Sunday titles designed by Paul Fuller

**77** Photograph by Jeremy Leslie

**78/9** Designed by Paul Fuller

**82/3** Actua Soccer 2 by Gremlin Interactive

**84/5** Courtesy of the artists

**86** CD inserts designed by Jim Phelan

**87** CD insert designed by Mark Farrow

**88** Lent by Jim Phelan

**89** Record sleeve designed by Peter Saville Associates

**94** Photograph by Jeremy Leslie

**95** Photograph by Nadav Kander

**Back cover** From top: Match of the Day television titles (p76); Coca Cola ad (p53); National Lottery scratchcard (p22); Sky television graphics (p79); *Striker* magazine masthead (p79); FC Porto scarf (p31).

**The authors**

Jeremy Leslie runs his own design studio in London.
Patrick Burgoyne is deputy editor of leading monthly communication arts magazine *Creative Review*.

This illustration shows Moses and Aaron promising food to the hungry Israelites. It comes from a fourteenth-century French Bible. In this illustration, as in many others, Moses appears to have horns. This is entirely due to a mistake in the earliest translation of the Hebrew Bible into Latin. When Moses came down from Mount Sinai, he should have been described as radiant. The mistake in translation implied that he had grown horns.

## Moses and God

When God first called Moses he was afraid and hid his face. However, he recovered quickly and was able to voice his doubts about the mission to Egypt. When his first meeting with Pharaoh was unsuccessful, Moses complained to God that He had broken his promise to deliver the Israelites from slavery. When God threatened to destroy the people after they had built the golden calf, Moses pleaded with him to change his mind.

## How do Jewish people regard Moses?

Moses remains very special to Jewish people. They respect Moses because he was chosen by God to help them. Jewish people call Moses *Moshe Rabbenu*, which means 'Moses, our teacher'. This is because he brought the Torah from God and taught it to the waiting Israelites.

'Never again did there arise in Israel a prophet like Moses — whom the Lord singled out, face to face, for the various signs and portents that the Lord sent him to display in the land of Egypt, against Pharaoh and all his courtiers and his whole country, and for all the great might and awesome power that Moses displayed before all Israel.'

Deuteronomy 34: 10–12

Of all the prophets, it was Moses who was given the ultimate privilege of receiving God's laws on the tablets of stone.

# Moses the leader

## Moses the prophet

Moses was one of many Jewish prophets. These were men and women chosen by God to speak for Him to try to persuade people to mend their ways.

All the prophets were good people, but Moses was special and was the most favoured by God. When Moses' brother and sister, Aaron and Miriam, criticized him, God reminded them how very special Moses was:

> 'Hear these My words: When a prophet of the LORD arises among you, I make myself known to him in a vision, I speak with him in a dream. Not so with My servant Moses: he is trusted throughout My household. With him I speak mouth to mouth, plainly and not in riddles, and he beholds the likeness of the LORD.'

Numbers 12: 6–8

## The covenant

Moses was the link between God and the Israelite people. When God gave Moses the Ten Commandments on Mount Sinai, He made an agreement with Moses as the representative of the Jewish people. This agreement, known as a covenant, was made with all Jewish people, not just with those

◀ The Jewish people keep the covenant alive today by obeying God's commandments. This family are keeping the commandment to remember the Sabbath day by walking to the synagogue for the morning service.

'Now then, if you will obey Me faithfully and keep My covenant, you shall be My treasured possession among all the peoples ... you shall be to Me a kingdom of priests and a holy nation.'

Exodus
19: 5–6

who were present at Mount Sinai at that time, but with all those from the generations to follow.

As His part of the agreement, God promised to take care of the Jewish people. In return the Jewish people had to promise that they would obey God's commandments. Jews are sometimes called the Chosen People. The Jews were not chosen by God because they were a large or powerful nation. They were chosen because they were willing to follow God's laws.

# Moses, the teacher

## The Ten Commandments

Seven weeks after they had fled from Egypt, God ordered Moses to tell the people to get ready, because he wanted to speak to them. Three days later they saw that Mount Sinai was covered by thick smoke. The mountain trembled. There were great bursts of thunder and lightning and the constant blaring of air blown through a ram's horn. This dramatic build-up highlights the importance of what was to come.

God called Moses to the top of the mountain and gave him the Ten Commandments. These orders, taken by Moses to the waiting Israelites, became the starting point for the whole of Jewish law and for legal systems all over the world.

### THE TEN COMMANDMENTS

1. I am the Lord your God who brought you out of the land of Egypt.
2. You shall have no other gods beside Me.
3. You shall not swear falsely by the name of the Lord your God.
4. Remember the Sabbath day and keep it holy.
5. Honour your father and your mother.
6. You shall not murder.
7. You shall not commit adultery.
8. You shall not steal.
9. You shall not bear false witness against your neighbour.
10. You shall not covet your neighbour's house or anything that is your neighbour's.

Exodus 20: 2–14

▲ When God handed Moses the tablets of the law, He told him they were to be stored in an 'Ark' made from wood and gold.

## The 613 *mitzvot*

Although there were ten main commandments, 613 commandments were given altogether. In Hebrew, the commandments are called *mitzvot*.

There are many *mitzvot* about food and its preparation. They detail which foods Jews may eat (kosher) and those that are not allowed. Another group of *mitzvot* deals with *tzedaka*: how Jews should help those in need. Helping others plays a large part in the life of any Jewish community.

Orthodox Jews follow the *mitzvot* as they are written and believe that doing this will strengthen their connection to God. They believe that the *mitzvot* are written in the words of God and must not be altered.

Modern followers of Judaism think that the *mitzvot* were written by men who were inspired by God. But, because they do not accept that the *mitzvot* are written in the actual words of God, they believe that they can be reinterpreted and adapted to a modern way of life.

▲ Hasidic Jews in Jerusalem, Israel. The Hasidic movement began in Poland in the eighteenth century and its members are ultra orthodox. They continue to dress in the Eastern European costume of their original leaders.

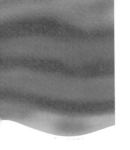

# The Sacred Texts

## The Tenakh

The Jewish Bible is called the *Tenakh*, and it has three parts: the Torah (the Five Books of Moses); *Nevi'im* (the books of the Prophets) and *Ketuvim* (the Writings).

The *Tenakh* gets its name from the first letters of the title of each of the three sections: TNK. The *Tenakh* is sometimes called the Written Law.

### The Torah

The Five Books of Moses are the most important books of the *Tenakh* because they contain the laws of Judaism and because they tell the story of how Judaism began.

The book of Genesis is about the creation of the world, Noah's flood and the lives of the Patriarchs: Abraham, Isaac and Jacob. Exodus tells how God guided Moses to rescue the people of Israel from Egypt and how they received God's holy law. Leviticus outlines many of the laws. In Numbers, Moses deals with uprisings and wars and sets up a council of elders to help him lead the people.

◄ The Torah is so important it is treated with great reverence.

The last of the five books, Deuteronomy, is Moses' farewell to the people. Before his death, Moses repeats the laws and teaching revealed in the first four books.

## The Torah and the Bible

The Five Books of Moses are also part of the first section of the Bible which is called the Old Testament. Jewish people do not use the term Old Testament because the second part of the Bible, the New Testament, is not part of Jewish scripture.

This father is teaching his son to read the Torah from a printed version called a Chumash. People use a Chumash for study purposes and for following the Torah reading in the synagogue. ▼

### READING THE TORAH

The Five Books of Moses have been divided into fifty-four sections. Each of these sections is called a *sidra*. A *sidra* is read each week at the synagogue, during the Shabbat morning service and on Monday and Thursday mornings. In the course of a year each of the fifty-four sections will have been read.

Although Jewish people speak of 'reading' from the Torah, the *sidra* is actually chanted rather than read. When the passage is finished, the Torah scroll is lifted up and the congregation says: 'And this is the Torah, which Moses set before the children of Israel, according to the commandment of the Lord by the hand of Moses.'

## Nevi'im (Prophets)

The story of the Jewish people is continued in the books of
the Early Prophets. After the death of Moses, Joshua
(Moses' assistant) led the Jewish people across the River
Jordan into Canaan, the Promised Land. A monarchy was
set up and the people were ruled by three powerful kings:
Saul, David and Solomon. After Solomon's death, the
country was divided into the kingdoms of Judah and Israel.

The first book of the Later Prophets is the Book of Isaiah.
This contains the famous prophecy of Isaiah: that one day
everyone will live in peace and harmony and there will be
no more war.

▲ Before Moses died, he asked
God to appoint a new leader.
God instructed him to find
Joshua and place his hand upon
him. This action showed the
transfer of leadership from
Moses to Joshua.

A passage from Prophets, called the *haftarah,* is read aloud in the synagogue after the reading of the *sidra.*

## *Ketuvim*

*Ketuvim* means 'the writings' and it is a collection of fourteen different books. *Ketuvim* begins with the Book of Psalms. The Book of Psalms is a series of songs written in praise of God. There are 150 psalms in all, and it is thought that almost half of them could have been written by King David. Moses himself might even have written Psalm 90, which is headed 'A prayer of Moses, the man of God.' Psalms play an important part in synagogue services.

Many of the other books of *Ketuvim* continue the history of the Jews. Some of these books are read in the synagogue on specific festivals. The Book of Esther, the story of a brave Jewess who became a queen of Persia, is read on the festival of Purim.

When people tell the story of Jonah, they usually say that he was swallowed by a 'whale'. The Bible actually says that Jonah was swallowed by a big fish. ▼

### PROPHETS

God chose many men and women to become prophets and speak to the people on his behalf. This was not always an easy or a comfortable thing to do. A man called Jonah did not want to be a prophet at all. He ran away from the responsibility and was caught in a terrible storm at sea, thrown overboard and swallowed, as the story goes, by a whale. Eventually he came safely to the shore and carried out the task that God had set him. He went to the city of Nineveh and persuaded the people there to pray that God would forgive their wickedness.

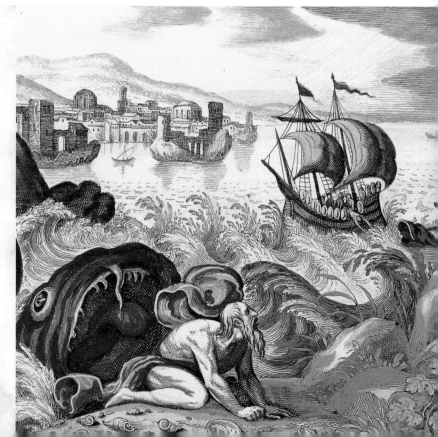

# The writings of the rabbis

## The Talmud

The Talmud is a record of the studies of the early rabbis, who discussed how God's holy laws should be followed. The Talmud has two parts: the Mishnah and the Gemara.

## The Mishnah and the Gemara

Mishnah means 'to learn or to teach by repetition'. The Mishnah was put together by Rabbi Judah the Prince at the beginning of the third century CE. Jews were being forced from their homeland in large numbers and Rabbi Judah recorded the discussions and rulings of the rabbis

### THE RABBI

Rabbi means 'my master' or 'my teacher'. The title of rabbi used to be given to anyone who knew a lot about Jewish law. Today a rabbi has to complete an official course of study. Rabbis still spend a lot of time teaching and explaining points of Jewish law. They may lead the synagogue service, or a cantor or member of the congregation may do it. Women are able to become rabbis of non-Orthodox communities.

This rabbi works in a Reform (non-Orthodox) congregation. She carries out exactly the same duties as her male colleagues. There are no women rabbis in Orthodox Judaism. ▶

so that the all Jews, wherever they lived, would follow the same traditions. The Mishnah covers the whole of Jewish law, from laws about land and crops to those that deal with cleanliness and the burial of the dead. The Gemara is a detailed discussion of the Mishnah.

## The Midrash

The Midrash is a collection of writings by rabbis, many of them stories, that explain something in the *Tenakh*. This could be an event or a commandment. The word midrash means 'enquiry'. A famous midrash explains how Moses got his stutter.

When Moses was a small boy his loyalty was tested by Pharaoh. A precious jewel and a pan of hot coals were placed together on a table and Moses was led towards them. Pharaoh's advisors had told him that if Moses took the jewel, it would mean that one day he would try to take Pharaoh's throne. It would prove that Moses was not to be trusted and that he should be killed. Moses started to reach for the jewel, but an angel nudged his hand towards the pan of coals. Moses picked up a hot coal, touched his mouth with it, burnt his lips and tongue and became 'slow of speech and slow of tongue'.

▲ Wherever they are, Jewish people will gather to study. This study session took place in Warsaw, Poland, during the Second World War. Early in the war the Nazis herded 500,000 Jews into a ghetto and imprisoned them behind a high brick wall. Even as many were dying from starvation or diseases, religious study still took place.

# Parchment scrolls

## Sefer Torah

In synagogues, the Torah is read from a scroll called the Sefer Torah. The Five Books of Moses that make up the Torah are the holiest of all Jewish scriptures and a Sefer Torah is always treated with great care and respect. The Sefer Torah will have a beautiful velvet or wooden cover and other rich ornaments.

A Torah scroll is made from pieces of parchment that have been sewn together to form a single scroll that is about 60 metres long. This long scroll is wrapped around wooden poles that have been attached to each end. The poles are used to unwind the scroll as it is being read. Whilst he or she is reading from the Torah, the reader will point to the words with a finger-shaped pointer called a *yad*. This is so the scroll is not touched unnecessarily.

The Torah is hand-written on the scroll in 250 vertical columns. This is slow and careful work and a scroll will probably take as long as a year to make.

▲ The Sefer Torah is the most sacred of all Jewish objects. When the writing on the scroll has faded so much that it can no longer be read, the scroll is buried with great respect.

The scrolls are kept in the synagogue, in a special cupboard called the Ark. The congregation stands as a mark of respect whenever the Sefer Torah is taken from the Ark.

## Mezuzah

Mezuzah is the Hebrew word for doorpost. It is the name given to a small piece of parchment that has the first two paragraphs of the *Shema* written on it (see page 5). This piece of parchment is rolled into a small, decorative container and fixed to the right-hand doorposts of rooms in a Jewish home. It is a constant reminder of God's presence and commandments.

## Tefillin

Like the mezuzah, tefillin remind the wearer of God's commandments. Tefillin are two small black leather boxes with straps. The first two paragraphs of the *Shema* and two passages from Exodus are written on parchment scrolls in each of the boxes. Orthodox Jewish men wear tefillin while reciting their morning prayers. One of the boxes is worn on the centre of his forehead and the other on his left arm.

▲ The mezuzah is placed in its case and fixed in the upper third of a doorpost.

▼ A Jewish boy will start to use tefillin during morning prayer after he has had his bar mitzvah (see pages 36–7). Tefillin are not used on Shabbat and festivals because it is thought that no further reminder of the covenant is needed.

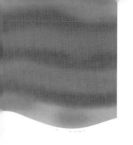

# Sacred and Special Places

## The Promised Land and the holy city

The land of Israel has been at the heart of Judaism since the religion began. God promised Abraham the land of Canaan for himself and his descendants. Moses led the children of Israel back towards this Promised Land after the hardship of their time as slaves in Egypt.

▲ Much of Israel's fertile land is now used to grow many different kinds of fruit.

### THE PROMISED LAND

'For the LORD your God is bringing you into a good land, a land with streams and springs and fountains issuing from plain and hill: a land of wheat and barley, of vines, figs and pomegranates, a land of olive trees and honey: a land where you may eat food without stint, where you will lack nothing…'

Deuteronomy 8: 7–8

## The land of Israel

Jewish people have not always had control over the land that is now called Israel and for much of their history many Jews have lived outside Israel. But Jewish writings and prayers show that they never forgot their Promised Land and always longed to return. Each time that Orthodox Jews recite a special prayer after they have eaten, they say: 'And rebuild Jerusalem the holy city, speedily and in our day.'

## Jerusalem

The holy city of Jerusalem was built on the site of a fortress captured by King David and is sometimes called the 'City of David'. David's son, Solomon, carried out his father's plan to build a temple there and made Jerusalem the capital of his kingdom. This temple (the First Temple) was destroyed in about 586BCE and the

Jews were forced into exile in Babylon. The Temple was later rebuilt (the Second Temple) and destroyed again, this time by the Romans in 70CE. Jews were expected to travel to Jerusalem three times a year to celebrate the festivals of Pesach, Shavuot and Sukkot while the Temple was still standing. These three festivals are called Pilgrim Festivals. Jerusalem has very special importance for Christians and Muslims as well as for Jews. Pilgrims of all these faiths travel to Jerusalem to visit their holy places.

Sacred Jewish, Muslim and Christian buildings contribute to the special beauty of Jerusalem. The rabbis say that ten measures of beauty came into the world and that, of these ten, Jerusalem took nine. ▼

# Jewish pilgrimage sites in Israel

## The Western Wall

All that remains of the First and Second Temples in Jerusalem today is a part of the wall that was built around the Temple Mount in the first century BCE. This is the most sacred Jewish site. For many centuries Jewish people have come to the Wall to mourn the loss of the Temple and, because of the sound of their crying, it is sometimes called the Wailing Wall.

Today a space has been cleared in front of the Wall for religious services. Bar and bat mitzvah ceremonies are often held there (see pages 36–7).

Visitors often write prayers on pieces of paper and push them between the gaps in the stones, in the hope that prayers sent from such a holy place will be answered favourably.

These boys are being taken to the Western Wall as part of their preparation for bar mitzvah (see page 36). ▼

## Burial sites

There are many sacred burial sites in Israel and the surrounding area. The oldest and largest Jewish cemetery in the world is on the Mount of Olives in Jerusalem. Jews have been buried here for more than 2,000 years. This cemetery is the holiest of all burial sites for Jews.

The Tomb of King David is also in Jerusalem. It was built in the Middle Ages and it is unlikely that it marks David's real burial place, but it has become a site of pilgrimage and prayer. The Patriarchs, Abraham, Isaac and Jacob, are thought to have been buried at the Cave of Machpelah in Hebron.

These sites, as well as the graves of many famous rabbis, are holy places where people come to pray to God. They sometimes leave written prayers at these holy places as they do at the Western Wall.

▲ The Mount of Olives used to be covered by olive trees. Instead of flowers, Jewish people place a small stone on a grave as a sign that they have visited.

### THE DEATH OF MOSES

Rabbinical legend says that as Moses died he was kissed by God. Moses has no known burial place.

'So Moses the servant of the LORD died there in the land of Moab, at the command of the LORD. He buried him in the valley of the land of Moab, near Beth-peor; and no one knows his burial place to this day.'

Deuteronomy 34: 5–6

◄ The Children's Memorial at Yad Vashem was hollowed out from an underground cavern.

# Places to remember the Holocaust

## Yad Vashem

Yad Vashem is Israel's memorial to those who died in the Holocaust. It is a large complex built on the Mount of Remembrance in Jerusalem with exhibition halls, museums and special collections of art and information about the Holocaust. The names of those who died are displayed here and there is a special and very sad memorial to all the children who died. The memorial candles placed there are reflected in the darkness and look like stars shining in a dark sky.

## The Anne Frank house

Before the Second World War, Anne Frank was a lively Jewish schoolgirl living in Amsterdam. When the Nazis invaded Holland Anne and her family were in great danger. Her father made plans for them to hide in a secret apartment above his office. In 1942, with the help of trusted friends, the Frank family disappeared from view. They remained hidden for two years. They were betrayed in August 1944, captured by the Germans and sent to a death camp. Anne died just two months before the end of the war.

Her father survived and after the war returned to Amsterdam where he found Anne's diary. The diary was published and Anne became famous. Today her hiding place, the Secret Annexe, is a museum. Thousands of people from all over the world, Jewish people especially, visit her former hiding place out of respect for her memory.

## Memorial sites across the world

There are memorials to the Holocaust victims all over the world. The former death camp of Auschwitz-Birkenau (in Poland) has become a museum memorial to those who were murdered there, as have many of the other camps. There is a Holocaust Memorial Museum in Washington, USA, and an underground memorial crypt in Paris. A museum in Copenhagen tells a happier story. It shows how most Danish Jews were helped to escape to safety in Sweden.

▲ Anne's family shared their cramped hiding place with another four people. Otto Frank, Anne's father, was the only one of the eight inhabitants of the Secret Annexe to survive. His younger daughter's diary has been translated into more than fifty languages and is read all over the world.

# Special Occasions and Festivals

Jewish people celebrate many festivals, spread out through the Jewish calendar. The Sabbath, or Shabbat, is a special day that is celebrated every week by Jewish families.

## Shabbat

The Jewish Sabbath is called Shabbat. Shabbat is the only festival or special day mentioned specifically in the Ten Commandments. It is a day that is set apart from the rest of the week. When Jews rest and pray on Shabbat, they remember that God rested on the seventh day after He created the universe. They also remember that they have the freedom to rest on Shabbat because God rescued them from slavery. Shabbat begins just before sunset on a Friday evening and ends at nightfall on the following day.

## Celebrating Shabbat

Friday evening is a time of celebration in a Jewish home. Orthodox Jews will not do anything that could be classed as work during Shabbat, such as switching on electricity or driving a car. Even families who do not follow all the customs will usually treat Friday evening as different and will gather together to enjoy a special meal. In a traditional home, Shabbat begins when the woman of the house lights the Shabbat candles and

◀ The two Shabbat candles represent the two parts of the fourth commandment, to 'remember' the Sabbath day and to 'keep it holy'.

recites the blessing. In a family with children, the father will bless his children, placing his hands over each child's head as he does so. Then it is time for the Kiddush, a blessing recited over a cup of wine, thanking God for the gift of Shabbat. A further blessing is made over two plaited loaves of bread called challah.

Many families attend synagogue services on Shabbat mornings. The high point of the morning service is when the Sefer Torah is taken from the Ark for the reading of the week's *sidra*.

### CHALLAH

Challah is a type of bread, and is always used on Shabbat and festivals. There are two loaves on the table at Shabbat, as a reminder of the Israelites' desert trek. While they were in the desert, God gave them a food called manna, which was like 'a wafer made with honey'. On the sixth day of the week, God sent them a double portion. This gave them enough to eat on the sixth day and on the seventh, which was Shabbat.

The two loaves are held while the blessing is recited. At the end, everyone responds by saying 'Amen'. The bread is then cut and everyone is given a slice. ▶

## 36

▲ A bar mitzvah at the Western Wall. The boy has completed his reading and has been lifted on to his father's shoulders as the family sing and dance in celebration.

A boy making a speech at the party that is being held to celebrate his bar mitzvah. He will pay tribute to his parents, grandparents and teachers. ▼

# Rites of Passage

## Bar mitzvah

When a boy reaches the age of thirteen, he will celebrate his bar mitzvah. The ceremony usually takes place on the Shabbat that follows his thirteenth birthday. It marks the fact that, in the eyes of his religion, the boy has become a man. Bar mitzvah means 'son of the commandment' and the boy should now observe all the Jewish laws. He can take his place as an official member of a minyan, the group of ten men who must be gathered before a service can take place. A boy will now wear his tefillin for morning prayers.

During the synagogue service, the bar mitzvah boy will recite a blessing on the Torah. He will go on to read some or all of the *sidra* and sometimes the *haftarah* or other parts of the service as well. He will have studied very hard to get to this point.

A bar mitzvah is a time for great celebration. The proud parents will give a party and the boy will receive many presents. His parents and grandparents will usually try to give gifts that he will keep always: a tallit (prayer shawl), tefillin or his own kiddush cup.

## Bat mitzvah

Bat mitzvah means 'daughter of the commandment'. Bat mitzvah ceremonies take place when a girl is twelve. Twelve has always been the age when a Jewish girl is considered to have reached adulthood, but it has only become usual to mark this with a ceremony in recent years.

A girl will attend special classes for some time before a bat mitzvah and study the *mitzvot* and Jewish history. She will spend a lot of time learning how to run a Jewish home.

A bat mitzvah ceremony taking place in a non-Orthodox synagogue. It is held in the same way as a bar mitzvah. The girl is wearing a prayer shawl and is reading from a Sefer Torah. ▼

There is not really a set pattern to the ceremony, but it will always include the Torah passage that begins 'A woman of worth who can find? For her price is beyond rubies', (Proverbs 31: 10–11), as a reading or a song.

Reform and Progressive branches of Judaism treat boys and girls in exactly the same way and a bat mitzvah ceremony is held during the regular Shabbat morning service in these congregations.

# Festivals

## Pesach

This festival, also called 'Passover', takes place in spring and lasts for eight days. It is the festival of freedom, the time when the Jewish people remember the exodus from Egypt and thank God for releasing them from slavery. As Jewish people celebrate, they should feel as if they themselves had been rescued from Egypt and set free.

## *Hametz*

On the night that Moses lead the Israelites out of Egypt, they made bread for their journey. They had to leave so quickly that there was no time to wait for the bread to rise. Jewish people remember this by avoiding *hametz* (leavened foods) during Pesach. They do not eat anything made from grain products that have risen or fermented and will eat matzah instead of bread at this time. Matzah is a flat, unleavened bread made from special flour and water, rather like a cracker or crispbread.

▲ Any last crumbs of *hametz* are gathered together and burnt before Pesach. As it burns, the head of the household recites a blessing.

Matzah dough is baked within 18 minutes to make sure it will not have any time to rise. ▶

Some utensils can be made kosher for use during Pesach by immersing them completely in boiling water. ▶

## Cleaning for Pesach

Not only do Jewish people avoid eating leavened foods, but they also avoid using anything that might have come into contact with them. Every trace of leavened food has to be removed from the house before Pesach. The house is spring-cleaned very thoroughly. The crockery, cutlery and kitchen equipment that is usually used is put away and sets that are only ever used during Pesach are brought out instead.

## Pesach cookery

Jewish families all have their favourite foods for Pesach. There are many delicious recipes for special cakes and biscuits. Different communities have slightly different customs. Sephardi Jews (Jews from Spain, Portugal and the Arab countries) continue to eat rice during Pesach. They also eat vegetables such as peas or beans that grow in pods. Ashkenazi Jews (Jews from Northern, Central and Eastern Europe) do not eat these foods during Pesach.

### SEARCHING FOR HAMETZ

However careful a family has been to remove all *hametz* from the house, they will search the house again on the evening before Pesach. This search is called *bedikat hametz*. Somebody will hide some pieces of bread around the house before the search begins. The search will not be over until all the pieces have been found. In this way the family can be absolutely sure that they have made a thorough search for every trace of the *hametz*.

## What is Seder?

The Seder is the service and evening meal celebrated at home on the first two nights of Pesach. Seder means 'order' and on Seder nights everything is done in a particular and unchanging order. The service is divided into two parts by a special meal. Families gather together for the Seder and invite guests to join them who would otherwise be alone. Seder involves the whole family and is at the heart of the celebration of Pesach.

## At the table

The Seder service is read from a book called a Hagadah. This means 'telling'. Many are brightly coloured with beautiful illustrations. The youngest child at the table is

Three pieces of matzah are placed on the Seder table. The middle piece is broken into two and half of it is used for the *Afikomen* (see page 41). After the traditional blessing everyone is given some of the top matzah and the remaining middle half to eat. ▼

▲ A Hagadah illustration that goes with a traditional Seder song called 'One Kid'.

given the job of asking four questions about why the Seder night is different from all other nights. The answers to the questions are given in the 'telling' of the story of how Moses was sent by God to lead the Israelites out of slavery in Egypt.

A Seder plate is placed on the table. It has a number of sections for special foods that also help to tell the story. Everyone must taste the *Haroset* (a mixture of apples, nuts, cinnamon and sugar, that is meant to look like the mortar which the Israelite slaves used in building), and the bitter herbs that represent the bitterness of slavery.

During the Seder everyone will drink four cups of wine. (Children will have a tiny cup, or wine mixed with water.) Each cup of wine stands for one of the four promises that God made to the Israelites: 'I will free you', 'I will deliver you', 'I will redeem you' and 'I will take you to be my people'. The Seder evening is long, but everyone enjoys the familiar songs that are sung at the end of the meal.

The Seder takes Jews back to a time when they suffered greatly, but by the end of the evening they start to look forward to a time when everyone will enjoy peace and freedom. The Seder celebration ends with the cry 'Next year in Jerusalem!'

▲ In some families everyone will take it in turns to read aloud from the Hagadah.

## THE AFIKOMEN

*Afikomen* means 'dessert'. It is the last piece of matzah that is eaten at the Seder. It stands for the last, hurried meal that the Israelites ate before they fled from Egypt. During the evening a father hides the *Afikomen* and the children will have to find it after dinner. The Seder cannot be finished until the *Afikomen* has been found and eaten. The finder gets a reward, as do all the other children who joined in the search!

# Shavuot, Sukkot and Simchat Torah

Sukkot is also the autumn harvest festival. The overhanging branches of the sukkah are decorated with autumn fruits, leaves and fragrant plants. These remain in place throughout the festival. ▼

## Shavuot

The two-day festival of Shavuot, 'the Season of the Giving of Our Law', celebrates the giving of the Torah to Moses on Mount Sinai. The Ten Commandments are read in the synagogue on the first day. Shavuot comes seven weeks after Pesach and is sometimes called the 'Feast of Weeks'.

It is also a harvest festival because it marks the beginning of the summer wheat harvest. On Shavuot it has become customary to eat dairy foods, especially cheesecake, to remember the promise of the 'land of milk and honey'.

## Sukkot

Sukkot commemorates the protection of God during the time that the Jewish people were wandering in the desert. Observant families build a sukkah to use during this eight-day festival in memory of the shelters that the Jews had to build in the desert. A sukkah is a shelter or hut, with three or four sides. Its roof is covered with cut branches and left partly open to the sky. The family will eat and even sometimes sleep in the sukkah.

## THE FOUR SPECIES

Four plants are used during prayer on Sukkot: the palm, myrtle, willow and *etrog*. They are known as the Four Species. The palm branch, myrtle and willow are wound together to form a bundle called a *lulav*. This is held in the right hand. An *etrog*, a yellow fruit that is rather like a lemon, is held in the left hand. At set times during the celebration, the *lulav* is waved in all directions to show that God is everywhere and that He showers His blessings from all sides.

## Simchat Torah

On Simchat Torah, 'the Rejoicing of the Law', the annual cycle of Torah readings comes to an end with the last verses of the Book of Deuteronomy. The readings immediately begin again with the first verses of Genesis.

The festival shows the love that Jewish people have for God's law. Simchat Torah is celebrated with all the joy of a wedding and the Torah readers on Simchat Torah are known as Bridegrooms of the Law. The Sefer Torah is carried around the synagogue, and sometimes outdoors, with much singing and dancing.

▲ To worship during Sukkot, people try hard to find the freshest and most perfect plants available. The *lulav* has to be green, its ribs should still be tight and it must come to a point at the top. The *etrog* must be yellow and its skin should be blemish-free.

# Judaism Today

## Where Jews live

There are approximately 15 million Jewish people today. They live in countries all over the world and come from different racial groups. They may be Ashkenazi (from Northern, Central and Eastern Europe), Sephardi (from Spain, Portugal and the Arab countries), Oriental (from ancient communities such as India and Yemen) or Beta Israel (from Ethiopia).

▲ Most of the ancient Jewish community of Ethiopia was rescued from persecution in the later part of the twentieth century.

The Jewish population of Europe fell dramatically during the Holocaust, when one-third of the world's Jewish population was killed, and the largest numbers of Jews now live in the United States and Israel.

### The State of Israel

Jews had prayed for a return to their homeland ever since they were forced to leave it. In the nineteenth century the Zionist movement was formed. Its aim was the re-establishment of a Jewish homeland. The State of Israel was founded in 1948 and, after the horror of the Holocaust, a second exodus began.

Israel's 'Law of Return' gives every Jew the right to live in Israel and to become an Israeli citizen. The most recent group of new citizens has come from the former Soviet Union. Israel today is home to Jews from all over the world: Europe, the United States, the Arab countries, Ethiopia and beyond.

## Jewish religious movements

There are now a number of Jewish religious movements. They fall into two main groups, Orthodox and non-Orthodox. Orthodox Jews follow traditional religious rules and customs. Some Orthodox Jews belong to Hasidic groups that are strictly observant. The Lubavitch group is one of the largest Hasidic groups. Lubavitch Jews run many education programmes and try to encourage other Jews to become more observant.

There are different non-Orthodox movements in different countries. These groups are not quite the same, but, unlike some Orthodox Jews, they all share a belief that Judaism can be adapted to meet the needs of a changing world.

These Orthodox Jewish men are celebrating at the Western Wall. The area near the wall is divided into two sections according to Orthodox tradition, providing a space for women and a separate space for men. ▼

## Moses and Judaism today

The Torah is the heart of Judaism. This is true for all branches of Judaism, Orthodox and non-Orthodox. All that is different is how they understand and explain it.

Moses has a special place in Judaism, because he was its greatest prophet and the very first Torah teacher. When Moses came down from Mount Sinai and told the people about God's commandments he began the traditions of Judaism that have continued for thousands of years to this day.

# Glossary

**Ark** The cupboard in a synagogue in which the Torah scrolls are kept.

**Bar mitzvah** A ceremony that is held to welcome a Jewish boy into the adult community.

**Bat mitzvah** A ceremony that is held to welcome a Jewish girl into the adult community.

BCE Before Christian Era.

**Cantor** The person who leads the prayers during a service in a synagogue.

CE Christian Era.

**Commandment** A rule or order given by God.

**Covenant** An agreement or contract, as in the agreement between God and the Israelites.

**Exodus** A mass departure of people.

**Ghetto** A part of a town where Jews were forced to live.

**Hagadah** The book read at the Seder. It tells the story of the Jews' escape from slavery in Egypt.

*Hametz* Leavened food forbidden during Pesach.

**Hebrew** The language of the Jewish Bible and the traditional language of Jewish prayer. A modern version of Hebrew is the language of Israel.

**Holocaust** The persecution and mass-murder of the Jews by the Nazis between 1933 and 1945.

**Kiddush** A blessing said over a cup of wine at the start of Shabbat and festival meals.

**Kosher** Food which Jews are allowed to eat.

**Leavened** Food that has fermented and risen.

*Mitzvot* Commandments. Sometimes used to mean 'good deeds'.

**Observant** Observing the rules of a religion.

**Orthodox Judaism** Traditional Judaism.

**Patriarch** The male head of a family or tribe. Abraham, Isaac and Jacob are the Patriarchs of Judaism.

**Pesach** The festival which marks the escape of the Jews from slavery in Egypt.

**Pharaoh** A ruler of Ancient Egypt.

**Pilgrim** Someone who travels to a holy place for religious reasons.

**Plague** A large number of animals or insects, or a serious disease that causes great damage.

**Prophet** Someone who speaks for God and tells people what God wants.

**Purim** The festival that celebrates the time when Queen Esther saved the Jewish people at the time of King Xerxes II of Persia.

**Rabbi** A Jewish religious teacher and leader.

**Reform Judaism** A non-Orthodox Jewish movement that has made changes to old religious laws and customs to fit in with changing times.

**Sefer Torah** A hand-written Torah scroll.

**Shabbat** The Jewish Sabbath. It begins before sunset on Friday and ends at nightfall on Saturday.

*Shema* An important prayer and statement of belief.

*Sidra* A passage from the Torah read in the synagogue on Shabbat mornings.

**Synagogue** A building where Jewish people meet, pray and study.

**Talmud** A collection of commentary and discussion, written by the early rabbis, known as the Oral Law.

**Tefillin** Two leather boxes containing passages from the Torah, which Jewish men wear on their head and upper arm during morning prayer.

*Tenakh* The Jewish Bible.

**Torah** The Five Books of Moses, but can also mean the Jewish Bible or the whole of Jewish law and teaching.

*Yad* A finger-shaped pointer used when reading from a Sefer Torah in a synagogue.

# Further Information

## Books to read

*The Illuminated Haggadah* edited by Michael Shire (Frances Lincoln, 1998)

*Jewish Festivals Cookbook* by Ronne Randall (Hodder Wayland, 2001)

*Judaism* by Arye Forta (Heinemann Educational, 1995)

*Judaism* by Angela Wood (Franklin Watts, 1999)

*Religions of the World: Jewish World* by Douglas Charing (Hodder Wayland, 2001)

*Tanakh: a New Translation of the Holy Scriptures According to the Traditional Hebrew Text* (Jewish Publication Society: Philadelphia, 1985)

*The Torah* by Douglas Charing (Heinemann Educational, 1993)

*The Facts About Judaism* by Alison Cooper (Hodder Wayland, 2004)

## Websites

*Akhlah*
http://www.akhlah.com/
A site for Jewish children with information about the Torah, festivals, Israel and Hebrew.

*BBC Online: Religion and Ethics: Judaism*
http://www.bbc.co.uk/religion/religions/judaism/index.shtml
A useful reference site.

*Judaism 101*
http://www.jewfaq.org/
An online encyclopaedia of Judaism.

The website addresses (URLs) included in this book were valid at the time of going to press. However, because of the nature of the Internet, it is possible that some addresses may have changed, or sites may have changed or closed down since publication. While the authors and publishers regret any inconvenience this may cause the readers, no responsibility for any such changes can be accepted by either the authors or the publisher.

## Places to visit

### UK and Ireland

Most communities are happy to make arrangements for school parties to visit their synagogue. Synagogues will usually be listed in the phone directory. In case of difficulty, and for further information, contact the Board of Deputies of British Jews (020 7543 5400) or the Scottish Council of Jewish Communities (0141 577 8248).

### Museums

Jewish Museum, Albert Street, London NW1 7NB
Manchester Jewish Museum, 190 Cheetham Hill Road, Manchester M8 8LW
The Irish Jewish Museum, 3/4 Walworth Road, South Circular Road, Dublin 8

### Holocaust Education

Beth Shalom Holocaust Centre, Laxton, Newark, Nottinghamshire NG22 OPA

### Outside the UK

All over the world there are museums dedicated to the memory of those who died in the Holocaust and to the study of Judaism and the Jewish people. A very few are listed below.
Israel
  Jerusalem: Yad Vashem and The Israel Museum
  Tel Aviv: The Museum of the Diaspora
Europe
  Amsterdam: The Anne Frank House
USA
  Washington: The United States Holocaust Memorial Museum
  New York: The Jewish Museum and The Museum of Jewish Heritage
Australia
  Sydney: The Sydney Jewish Museum

# Index

The numbers in **bold** refer to photographs and maps, as well as text.